From the Library of Mike Cherrington

WAR
= ON THE =
NILE

MICHAEL BARTHORP

WAR
= ON THE =
NILE

BRITAIN, EGYPT AND THE SUDAN
1882·1898

BLANDFORD PRESS
POOLE · NEW YORK · SYDNEY

BY THE SAME AUTHOR FROM BLANDFORD PRESS
The Zulu War: A Pictorial History
The North-West Frontier – British India and
Afghanistan: A Pictorial History 1839–1947
British Infantry Uniforms Since 1660 (with artwork by
Pierre Turner)
British Cavalry Uniforms Since 1660 (with artwork by
Pierre Turner)

First published
in the UK 1984
by Blandford Press,
Link House, West Street,
Poole, Dorset, BH15 1LL

Reprinted 1986

Copyright © 1984 Michael Barthorp

Distributed in
the United States by
Sterling Publishing Co., Inc.,
2 Park Avenue, New York,
N.Y. 10016

Distributed in
Australia by
Capricorn Link (Australia) Pty Ltd,
PO Box 665, Lane Cove, NSW 2066

British Library Cataloguing in Publication Data

Barthorp, Michael
  War on the Nile.
  1. Egypt—History—British occupation,
  1882-1936   2. Egypt—History, Military
  3. Sudan—History—1862-1899   4. Sudan
  —History, Military
  I. Title
  962'.04   DT107.4

ISBN 0 7137 1310 0 (Hardback)
ISBN 0 7137 1858 7 (Paperback)

Typeset by Asco Trade Typesetting Ltd., Hong Kong
Printed in Great Britain by R.J. Acford Ltd., Chichester, Sussex.

CONTENTS

Foreword

A century ago Queen Victoria was within three years of her Golden Jubilee, Gladstone was Prime Minister for the second time, the agricultural population received the vote for the first time, a six-course dinner in a restaurant cost three shillings and sixpence, and the bustle had recently re-appeared on ladies' dresses after a brief demise. Outside England there was – as always – trouble in Ireland, a war was brewing in the Balkans and a rebellion in Canada, while in the United States, Grover Cleveland was about to begin the first of his two presidencies. France was advancing her empire in the Far East and Russia was again on the march in Central Asia; the former impelling Britain into a preventative campaign in Burma, the latter reviving old fears for the safety of India. But as the last quarter of 1884 moved inexorably towards 1885, what really gripped the attention of the British people, and indeed much of the civilised world, was the fate of one lone Englishman besieged for months by thousands of fanatical tribesmen in a distant desert town on the banks of a great river, where food was running out and his few doubtful soldiers of an unsoldierly race were hardly strong enough to lift their weapons. A relief column on camels and in rowing boats was fighting its way to reach him, but whether it would arrive in time was the question that perturbed everyone from the Queen downwards.

The epic defence of Khartoum by one of the great Victorian heroes, General Charles Gordon, and the belated endeavour to save him form the central section of this book. It is, or used to be, a familiar story – something every schoolboy knows – but it was only part of Britain's long involvement with Egypt and the Sudan, which began at the very end of the eighteenth century with Nelson's great victory of the Nile. Britain had no wish nor need to incorporate Egypt – let alone the Sudan – into her Empire, but when Egypt's instability bred of misgovernment gave rise to fears for the safety of Britain's Imperial communications through the Suez Canal, not to mention her investment in the country and her major shareholding in the Canal, Britain felt forced to intervene. This she did in 1882 – with rather more success than was to attend her efforts under not dissimilar circumstances in 1956. But through becoming involved in Egypt so too, inevitably and reluctantly, did she become involved with the Sudan (then an Egyptian province and in the grip of a massive rebellion against Egypt's misrule). Neither a nationalist military revolt in Egypt nor an enslaved people's uprising in the Sudan directly threatened, by armed might, the security of the British Empire but, as always, waiting in the wings were those other two great expansionist Powers of the period: Russia, eager for an outlet into the Levant at the expense of the Sultan of Turkey (Egypt's nominal overlord); and France, then building her African empire and with a long tradition of influence in Egypt. Though the Sudan had to be left to its own devices for over a decade after Gordon's ill-fated mission, basically it was the need to forestall French territorial ambitions that eventually drove Britain to reclaim the Sudan from the savagery and despotism into which it had fallen.

Thus Britain fought three wars in the deserts of Egypt and the Sudan – in 1882, in 1884–85 and 1896–98 – to protect her Imperial interests and, having done so, instituted measures to benefit the inhabitants of both countries. It was doubtless to her advantage to do so, but at the same time she gave to the Egyptians and Sudanese a more just, ordered and prosperous existence than she had found there, even though the later and natural growth of national aspirations in these countries ultimately, and

7

inevitably, earned her more opprobrium than gratitude. Furthermore, it is perhaps not too much to claim that had it not been for the position she gained at this vital cross-roads of three continents, by force of arms at Tel-el-Kebir and Omdurman, the outcome possibly of the First World War, and certainly the Second, might have been very different.

Here then is the story of these three campaigns and the men who endured heat and thirst and danger to fight them. On the one hand the story portrays three of the great Victorian military figures – Wolseley, Gordon and Kitchener – and on the other, it portrays the first Egyptian nationalist, Arabi Pasha; the compelling and fanatical Mohammed Ahmed, the Mahdi who believed himself destined to impose Islam upon the world; and his successor, the ruthless and cunning Khalifa Abdullah. Its participants include not only the Victorian Army, fighting the last of its 'little wars', but also the Royal Navy (afloat and ashore), sepoys and sowars from India, boatmen from Canada, volunteers from Australia and, in addition, two very contrasting Egyptian Armies, one of Turkish mould, as enemies, the other British-trained, as allies. Lastly and perhaps most remarkably it is the story of the tattered, half-naked Dervish hordes of the Sudan – the Baggara horsemen, the black Bazinger riflemen, the wild and ferocious Hadendoa, and countless men-at-arms from Darfur to the Red Sea – who hurled themselves unhesitatingly again and again, in expectation of a better life in the here-after, against the most lethal weapons that Victorian industry could devise.

To help the reader visualise these scenes and events as they appeared to the participants, the text is complemented by some 150 illustrations, some of them photographs, others contemporary paintings and drawings. Wherever possible the latter have been chosen from the work of eye witnesses to the events depicted, or by artists informed by such eye witnesses. These include, for example, the well-known military painter, R. Caton Woodville, whose battle pictures of earlier wars are famous for their inaccuracies but who was present in Egypt in 1882 as a war artist, recording what he actu-

ally observed; the even better-known Lady Butler, whose husband was on Wolseley's staff; and for the Sudan, two more war artists, Melton Prior and C.E. Fripp, as well as the former Indian Army officer, G.D. Giles. Some of these illustrations may be familiar, though others have never been reproduced before. Since this is predominantly a story of military operations, the illustrations are obviously in the main of a military nature but, since neither photography nor war artists were available to the Dervishes nor, come to that, to Gordon in Khartoum, the coverage is of necessity one-sided and uneven. As far as photographs of actual operations in the field are concerned, these are not extensive for earlier campaigns, due to the technical difficulties faced by a photographer – however intrepid – with the equipment then available. This is to some extent compensated for by a series in the Royal Collection of officers and men who took part, some of which are reproduced herein by gracious permission of Her Majesty the Queen. The second Suakin expedition of 1885 was accompanied by a photographic detachment of the Royal Engineers, whose chief task was to record the construction of the railway, but who also managed to capture a number of scenes and groups of members of the Field Force. By the time of the final campaign, the Kodak hand camera with roll-film had been developed (in 1888), so that scenes of much greater immediacy could quickly be 'snapped' by any officer who had such a camera, as indeed several did.

The inclusion of such a number of pictures, some not easily accessible, could not have been achieved without help and guidance. For this, the author is especially indebted to: Miss Frances Dimond of the Royal Archives; the staffs of the National Portrait Gallery, the National Maritime Museum, and the National Army Museum, notably Miss J.M. Spencer-Smith and Mrs M. Harding; the Home Headquarters, The Royal Hussars, Regimental Headquarters of The Staffordshire Regiment, The Duke of Edinburgh's Royal Regiment (Berkshire & Wiltshire) and The Queen's Own Highlanders (Seaforth & Camerons); Lieutenant-Colonel T.C. Sargent, late Australian

Army; Mr Peter Stanley of the Australian War Memorial; Mr Douglas Anderson; Mr R.G. Harris; and particularly to Mr R.J. Marrion. A special word of gratitude is due to Lieutenant-Colonel B.A.C. Duncan MBE, Royal Tank Regiment, for information about the Battle of Omdurman and the Dervish Army acquired while a member of the British Army Training Team in the Sudan. Lastly the author must thank his wife for sowing the seed and for reading the text; Mr Barry Gregory for his patience and encouragement; Mrs Sheila Watson for her kindly supervision of the author's interests; and the London Library for its efficiency and forbearance.

Jersey   M.J.B.
Channel Islands

Prologue: First Shots

Fifteen miles east from the ancient city of Alexandria, along the Egyptian shore, lies the fishing village of Aboukir dominated by an old fort out on a promontory. Its walls command the great sweeping curve of a bay cut out of the coastline and extending for thirty miles to the westerly mouth of the Nile at Rosetta. Here in this bay off Aboukir, on 1 August in the year 1798, a battle fleet lay at anchor in line astern facing north-west. From its masts flew the Tricolour of Republican France, for this was the squadron which had escorted General Napoleon Bonaparte's Army of the Orient to Egypt, an army which a week before had entered Cairo after defeating the Mameluke rulers of the country at the Battle of the Pyramids. While the soldiers of France celebrated their triumph, her sailors, moored at their anchorage, watched the Mediterranean with some unease. Somewhere over the horizon was another fleet, ships of the Royal Navy under the command of Rear-Admiral Sir Horatio Nelson.

To avoid the shoals which lined the coast, the French commander Admiral Brueys had anchored his line of thirteen battleships a mile and a half off-shore. His flagship, *L'Orient*, a huge three-decker with 120 guns, lay in the centre of the line which occupied about a mile of water, with the more powerful ships concentrated towards the rear which Brueys considered was most likely to be attacked. To add further support two frigates were stationed between the rearmost ships and the shore, while to protect the van a battery of mortars had been established on a small island in front of the fort at Aboukir. Another frigate, *Sérieuse*, lay between *Le Guerrier* in the van and the shore. Although the fleet mustered a total of 1182 guns the ships were undermanned, numbers of the crews being ashore digging for water or fetching supplies from Alexandria, and those that remained on

board were many of them inexperienced and poorly disciplined; a large number were little more than boys. If Nelson came, the fleet could put to sea and meet him in the open, but it was doubtful whether with such crews the ships could be sailed and the guns served at the same time. Therefore it seemed safer to remain at anchor with the port side protected by the shoals and the frigates, and to concentrate the available manpower on the starboard guns. By the early afternoon of 1 August, Brueys – a brave and able commander but suffering from dysentery – was still undecided which course of action to adopt, though he felt there would be time enough to decide once the British fleet was sighted.

At two o'clock the French look-outs reported sail on the horizon and by four Nelson's squadron was in full view, bearing down from the north: thirteen 74-gun ships of the line, the 50-gun *Leander* and a brig. With only three hours or so of daylight remaining, Brueys thought it unlikely that any action would occur that evening, but as the British ships came on under full sail with the wind behind them, he realised that Nelson did indeed intend to attack as soon as he was within range. He conferred hastily with his senior officers and although one recommended putting to sea immediately, his chief-of-staff, Ganteaume, urged that they should fight from anchor. Brueys gave the order to clear for action and for extra cables to be thrown out to secure the ships more firmly.

Aboard the British flagship HMS *Vanguard* Nelson, though afflicted by a nagging toothache, was in a fever of impatience and eagerness to be at the French. For over two months he had searched the Mediterranean for this fleet and now he had found it. During those weary weeks he had discussed with his captains over and over again how they would attack according to

Battle of the Nile, 1 August 1798. The start of the action in Aboukir Bay as Nelson's squadron bears down on the French van. Painting by N. Pocock.

the various possible dispositions of the enemy. Now, as the drums beat to quarters, the signal flags broke out indicating that it was the French van and centre to be attacked. Every captain knew what he had to do and each raced the other to be first at the foe. 'By this time tomorrow,' Nelson said, 'I shall have gained a peerage or be in Westminster Abbey.'

As the British seventy-fours bore down, *Zealous* and *Goliath* were in the lead when they came within range at about 6.15. At the last moment *Goliath* pulled ahead, and to resounding cheers from *Zealous*, Captain Foley crossed the head of the French line, intending to lay his ship alongside *Le Guerrier* on the landward side, anchoring by the stern. But the anchor did not pull him up until he was opposite the second French ship, *Conquérant*, on which he immediately opened fire with his port guns.

Captain Hood of *Zealous*, seeing that *Goliath* had successfully sailed between the French and the shore, followed the same course to attack *Le Guerrier*. As the broadsides of *Goliath* and *Zealous* thundered into the two leading Frenchmen, their course was followed by three more ships, HMS *Orion* (which sank the frigate *Sérieuse* in passing), *Theseus* and *Audacious*, so that the ill-prepared port sides of the first half-dozen French ships were now under heavy fire from five British seventy-fours.

With the French hotly engaged on the landward side, Nelson edged down to attack the seaward flank. As *Vanguard* anchored to engage the third French ship, HMS *Minotaur*, *Defence*, *Bellerophon* and *Majestic* sailed past to anchor ahead of her, opening fire with their starboard guns as they came opposite the centre ships of the French line. Thus there were now ten British ships attacking eight of the enemy's from both sides and between them.

Darkness soon fell though the bay was lit by the flashes of the constant broadsides. Near the

11

The assault landing of General Sir Ralph Abercrombie's army at Aboukir Bay, 8 March 1801. Detail of an engraving after P. de Loutherbourg.

Aboukir promontory, however, navigation was difficult and HMS *Culloden*, which had been some way behind the fleet, ran aground on the shoals and was unable to enter the fight. Her plight was observed by the two ships accompanying her, *Swiftsure* and *Alexander*, who altered course in time and bore down to take up station one on either side of the French flagship *L'Orient* whose guns had succeeded in disabling *Bellerophon*. Battle was now fully joined and in this once tranquil and lonely Egyptian bay the night was made hideous by the booming guns, the crash of falling masts and spars, the cheers and shouts of the living, the screams and groans of the dying.

Aboard *L'Orient* Admiral Brueys had suffered mortal wounds and at nine o'clock his great ship caught fire. Despite the flames, the French seamen continued to serve their guns on the upper deck, but the blaze increased in fury until at about ten the flagship blew up in a colossal explosion, its horrifying sight and sound stunning the crews of both sides. For a while the din and frenzy of the fight ceased, but soon the deadly work began again. Below deck on *Vanguard*, Nelson believed himself blinded and near death, having been wounded in the head a little earlier, but the pain and profusion of blood exaggerated the severity of his wound. Once it had been dressed, he continued to issue orders to ensure the total victory of his ships.

At about three in the morning, with the men of both fleets reeling from exhaustion, the endless flashes and deafening roar of the guns ebbed and died away. The French crews had fought like tigers but, attacked on both sides, six of their ships had been forced to strike, their flagship was destroyed and two more had run aground. One frigate was sunk, a second had blown up. Aboard the dismasted *Tonnant*, her

The Battle of Alexandria, 21 March 1801. The mortally wounded Abercrombie seated among his staff as his victorious troops rout the French. Engraving after P. de Loutherbourg.

gallant captain, Dupetit-Thouars, despite having suffered terrible wounds, had continued to command his ship, until such was his weakness from loss of blood that he blew his brains out rather than make a foolish decision. Of the British ships, none had been sunk or forced to submit but all had suffered severely in damage and casualties.

When the sun came up around five o'clock only three ships of the French rear under Rear-Admiral Villeneuve were able to continue the fight, but soon, seeing the battle was lost, Villeneuve cut his cables and made for the open sea. One ship ran aground so that, out of Brueys' original squadron, only two ships of the line and the two remaining frigates made their escape. Nelson and his battered ships were masters of Aboukir Bay, while far inland Bonaparte and his army were cut off from their homeland.

The Battle of the Nile, as Nelson styled it, had other far-reaching effects. The Sultan of Turkey,

the nominal suzerain of Egypt, declared war on France. The Tsar of Russia, already at war with France, sent a fleet into the Mediterranean to attack the French-held Ionian Islands and an army into Italy to bolster up the Austrians. Among the messages carrying the news of the French fleet's destruction and Bonaparte's predicament in Egypt was one borne eastwards to Bombay, where the British officials of the Honourable East India Company had been concerned that the French presence in Egypt was the first step on a long march that would ultimately invade the domains they held in trust for the British crown.

France under the Bourbons had once been powerful in India but that power had been crushed by England in the Seven Years War. Her Revolutionary masters, however, had perceived their opportunity to make trouble for their enemy, England, by intriguing with and rendering military aid to Indian native rulers who had not yet succumbed to the Company's rule. Up to 1798 the aid had been confined to the despatch of officers to train the native armies, but a French army in Egypt posed a far more serious danger, opening up the possibility of a French naval base in the Red Sea or even an advance eastwards overland. Although Nelson's victory had not altered the fact of the French land presence in Egypt, the destruction of its Mediterranean fleet, on which its communications with France depended, had dealt a heavy blow to French seapower and left Bonaparte's army in something of a vacuum. That the East India Company's directors slept easier in their beds after the Nile was manifested by a personal gift to Nelson of £10,000.

Bonaparte may have had a dream of using Egypt as a springboard to invade India, but whether he had any more concrete plan for doing so at the time seems unlikely. Certainly he recognised the strategic importance of Egypt and the Levant, from which 'le commerce des Indes' could be threatened. In 1797 he had told the Directors of the Republic, 'if we are effectively to destroy England, we must get hold of Egypt.' This he had indeed done, but with his fleet shattered, his effective control of Egypt confined to Cairo and Alexandria, his soldiers afflicted by homesickness and disease, his treasury empty, and Turkey making ready to advance against him, his hold on Egypt was illusory and certainly not likely to prove the death-blow to England that he had promised his troops it would be. His advance into Syria to counter the Turks was foiled at Acre by a stout-hearted defence led by an English naval captain and a French emigré colonel, whose efforts were aided by plague raging through Bonaparte's ranks. Though his subsequent return to Cairo was presented as a triumph and a Turkish landing at Aboukir was defeated, the fate of the Egyptian expedition, first signalled by Nelson's broadsides, drew ever closer to its inevitable doom. Bonaparte, however, would not be there to share it. Events in Europe and a political crisis in France beckoned him. Just over a year after the Nile, he abandoned the army to which he had promised glory, and secretly sailed for France, there to seize power as First Consul and subsequently Emperor. It was another two years before the Army of the Orient followed its leader home, 'not in glory but defeat'.

In March 1801 another British fleet stood off the scene of Nelson's victory at Aboukir. This time the men-of-war were accompanied by transports carrying an army under General Sir Ralph Abercrombie, come to rid Egypt of the French invaders. Early in the morning of 8 March the ships' boats, packed with red-coated infantry, were rowed to the shore where, amid the sandhills, could be seen the waiting French. Though under heavy fire the British troops stormed ashore and battled their way forward, driving the French from their positions until a beach-head was fully secured so that the rest of the army could be landed. In the weeks that followed, the French were defeated in a battle outside Alexandria, that city was besieged and Cairo occupied. The French troops, weary and disillusioned with their three-year sojourn in this ancient land, capitulated and were sent home.

Thus ended France's attempt to seize and hold Egypt by force of arms. But though her soldiers and sailors had failed, the cultural and technological influences bequeathed to the country during the French occupation – a legacy of the band of learned civilians that had accompanied Bonaparte's army – would prove far more significant and long-lasting. France may have been the first European power since Rome, apart from Turkey, to exert her authority over the land of Egypt, to reveal its antiquities and to spread the word of Western civilisation; and France's desire to maintain her influence would not diminish throughout the nineteenth century. But it was Britain, ever conscious of her communications with her eastern Empire, that would become the more-closely enmeshed with the affairs and destinies of the peoples of the Nile Delta and the desert wastes to the south. However, it would be more than eighty years after Nelson and Abercrombie before blue-jackets and redcoats sailed out of the west to land again on the Egyptian shore.

= PART I =

THE CLEANSING OF EGYPT

1

The Half-Way House

The basic problem of the Ottoman Empire, both for itself and for the great powers of Europe, was its size. From its nominal centre of authority, the Sublime Porte at Constantinople, its possessions at the close of the Napoleonic Wars in 1815 ranged north-west through the Balkans to within 200 miles of Vienna, embracing large parts of what are now Yugoslavia and Romania, as well as the whole of Albania, Bulgaria and Greece. South-eastwards, beyond Turkey proper, its rule extended to the Persian Gulf and around the entire Arabian peninsula before bending westwards to take in the Sudan, Libya and Tunis, thus enclosing within this vast periphery Egypt and the Levant. In religion the Sultan's subjects were Moslems, Christians and Jews; in race Turks, Slavs, Circassians, Greeks, Latins, Arabs, Armenians, Kurds and Negroes. Such diversity of lands and peoples inevitably contained the seeds of disintegration rather than cohesion, and when to this was added the geographical position of the Empire as the junction between Europe, Asia and Africa, enclosing the eastern end of the Mediterranean on one side and opening on to the Indian Ocean on the other, then the instability and decay of the great ramshackle edifice was of obvious concern to the great powers of Europe. The Eastern Question, as it was known, was a major threat to peace in Europe throughout the nineteenth century and would provide one of the causes of the Great War in 1914.

All the powers were affected by this problem to a greater or lesser degree, but none more so than Russia. Greece won her independence from the Sultan in 1829 and the desire for liberty from the Turkish yoke spread north among the Balkan Christians. Since most of these were Slavs of the Greek Church, the Tsar considered himself their champion and their destined liberator. Furthermore Russian eyes were permanently fixed on Constantinople and the Dardanelles as the only outlet into the Mediterranean from the Black Sea. Not only was Turkey in danger of being outflanked through the Balkans but also in the east where, during the 1820s, Russia began to expand into Persia through the Caucasus. Thus there loomed the possibility of the twin tentacles of Russian power extending through south-east Europe into the Levant and the Mediterranean, and through Asia towards the Indian Ocean, even unto India itself. Such a danger could not but be of concern to Britain with her eastern interests. To forestall the more distant threat, British forces entered Afghanistan in 1837, there to become embroiled in the First Afghan War. Her main line of communications at this time was still the seaward route round the Cape of Good Hope, but the French adventure into Egypt in 1798 had also focused British attention on the strategic importance of that country as a bridge between the Mediterranean and the Red Sea, affording a shorter, overland route.

Egypt had been a province of the Ottoman Empire since 1517, but Turkish authority over the country had been nominal, power residing in the hands of the Mameluke beys, or princes, a warrior caste descended from slaves imported from the Caucasus to serve as soldiers. They had ruled by the sword, fighting each other and their Turkish overlords, while collecting rent from the indigenous Egyptian peasants or *fellahin*. After the Mamelukes had been defeated by the French, and the latter ejected by the British, a period of anarchy followed until 1806 when power was seized by Mohammed (or Mehemet) Ali, a tough, formidable and ambitious Albanian, once an officer in the Ottoman Army. He routed a second British expedition sent to Egypt in 1807 and then set about eliminating what remained of the Mamelukes. Having ruthlessly subdued the country, he instituted reforms and improvements including a system of irrigation and the cultivation of cotton. Though his methods were autocratic in the extreme and at times ferocious, he acted always for the greater prosperity and aggrandisement of Egypt as a nation, rather than as a downtrodden province of the Sultan. With French help he built up a fleet and a large army, conquering the Sudan to the south in 1820, later leading his troops north into Palestine and Syria to threaten the Sultan who had reneged on certain promises made to him. His successes threw the European powers into a turmoil, and it was not until French support, hitherto steadfast, failed him in 1840, that he was forced to come to terms with the Sultan as his rightful overlord. In return he was recognised as hereditary Viceroy of Egypt and Governor of the Sudan. Under his rule Egypt began to take the first real steps in the transformation from a backward, oriental fiefdom into a modern state, a process that was

to be continued under his successors though, as will be seen, one that would benefit only a minority of the inhabitants, rather than the country as a whole.

No British military presence had remained in Egypt after the Napoleonic Wars, but in 1845 Mohammed Ali had allowed a Lieutenant Waghorn, an officer in the East India Company's Navy, to organise an overland route for mails and passengers between Alexandria and Suez to link up with a regular service of steamers from London and Bombay. By this means communications between London and India were reduced to thirty days, or less than one-third of the sailing time round the Cape. Twelve years later a desert railway from Cairo to Suez was operating and the latter had become an important port. With the acquisition of this second, speedier route to India, the security and stability

Different types of Egyptian men and women. Photograph *c* 1880.

Bird's eye view of the Canal passing from Suez, at bottom, through the Bitter Lakes, Lake Timsah and Ismailia (centre), to Port Said and the Mediterranean at top.

for the plight of the Sultan's Christian subjects, was unwilling to countenance any Russian expansion at the expense of the Ottoman Empire, nor did she wish to annex Egypt. As Lord Palmerston put it, 'I want a well-managed inn to serve as a half-way house on the way to my country place; but I don't want to buy the inn.' The Tsar's proposal was refused – to his bewilderment – and in due course Britain, allied with France, drifted into the Crimean War in defence of Turkey. As a result Russia was barred from Constantinople and incapacitated in the Black Sea. Egypt was undisturbed and Britain's fast route to India remained secure. This, however, was soon to undergo a crucial transformation.

Since 1798 France's interest and influence had been more pervasive in Egypt than that of any other power. From 1854 this increased materially with the arrival of many Europeans, but particularly French, following the accession to the Viceregal throne of Said Pasha, a descendant of Mohammed Ali, a benevolent but extravagant ruler, full of schemes for the modernisation of his country whose fulfilment required European expertise. Said delighted in his Europeans and one in particular, Ferdinand de Lesseps, a retired French consular official with a life-long personal ambition – to cut a canal through the Suez Isthmus to link the Mediterranean with the Red Sea. Having gained Said's ear, de Lesseps used all his undoubted powers of persuasion to acquire not only the concession to build the canal but also the forced labour for its construction, and considerable tracts of land on either side of its intended route. With the Viceregal approval in his pocket, de Lesseps set about forming his Suez Canal Company. He encountered many difficulties, hostility from Britain and prevarication from the Sultan but eventually the subscribers were found, many of them French, and four years after he had received the concession the Company was launched. Soon the great work began, to continue for ten years beset by delays and growing costs until its opening, amid scenes of enormously costly splendour, by the Empress Eugenie of France in 1869.

These ceremonies – the huge banquets, balls,

of Egypt became of vital importance to Britain. The chief external threat was obviously the Russian designs on the Balkans and Constantinople, and consequently British foreign policy was cast to bolster up the shaky, corrupt and frequently oppressive Ottoman Empire, while at the same time the Royal Navy stood ready at its bases in Gibraltar and Malta to act if diplomacy failed.

In 1854 fail it did. The Tsar Nicholas I, deciding that the time was ripe to settle the Eastern Question, proposed a partition of the Ottoman Empire, of which Britain's share would be Egypt and Crete. Britain, though not without sympathy

The harbour of Port Said at the northern end of the Canal.

fêtes and firework displays, the new opera *Aida* specially commissioned for the occasion, the great procession of ships led by European royalty, the fact of the Canal itself – may have put Egypt and its Court on the map but it had cost the Egyptian fellahin dear, in life and in taxes wrung from their meagre earnings by the kourbash, the rhinoceros-hide whip of the tax officials. Said had not lived to see the fulfilment of de Lesseps' dream, dying in 1863, but for his successor Ismail the opening of the Canal was the culmination of six years' most profligate expenditure and ostentatious display.

If ever there was a man obsessed with *idées de grandeur* it was Ismail Pasha of Egypt. Of uncouth appearance and of little learning, he nevertheless possessed considerable charm of manner, a persuasive tongue and, on the sur-face at least, an open-handed geniality. As a young man he had shown promise but on becoming Viceroy all his endeavours were directed to the portrayal of Egypt as a state comparable with any in Europe, not for the benefit of the Egyptians as Mohammed Ali, and to a lesser extent Said Pasha had done, but for the greater glorification, enrichment and self-indulgence of Ismail Pasha himself. He visited the Courts of Europe and in return invited his hosts to Cairo. The influx of Europeans that had begun under Said became a flood, either as tourists or as bankers, entrepreneurs, technicians of all sorts, all eager to benefit themselves in the further-ance of Ismail's grandiose schemes. But it was a sham, as pretentious as the false beards he

19

supplied to his palace bodyguard to render them as imposing as Queen Victoria's Yeomen of the Guard, as bogus as the veneer of European sophistication that masked the oriental despot Ismail really was. As the great modern buildings went up in Cairo and Alexandria, as Ismail's fortune grew and grew, so the lot of his people became more wretched and the national treasury more depleted.

Though delighting in the prestige the Canal gave him, Ismail had earlier demanded a revocation of many of the concessions so open-handedly granted by Said to the Canal Company. In its turn the Company, already under financial pressure, had demanded compensation and got it, being awarded £3 million by the arbitrator Napoleon III. Furthermore, to obtain immunity from any future claims, Ismail agreed to pay an equal sum to be realised from the dividends on his own Canal shares inherited from Said. The kourbash was plied more vigorously along the Nile as the wretched fellahin had more and more extracted from them: to pay for the Canal, to pay the Sultan for Ismail's new title of Khedive, to pay for Ismail's splendid, modern Egypt 'where French fashion, harem life and the abject misery of the fellahin jostle each other in a confusion'; the whole glittering facade concealing a miasma of tyranny, corruption, lethargy and squalor. There was, however, a limit to what could be wrung from Egypt, and in his voracious appetite for more money Ismail turned to the European bankers, men far more astute than he and only too ready to open their coffers at punishing rates of interest. As Ismail's stucco palaces and personal expenditure went up, so did his debt to the bankers who quietly bided their time, waiting for the moment to pounce. In 1875 pounce they did and Ismail was forced back on his only asset to pay the interest: he decided to sell his shares in the Canal.

When the project for the Canal was first mooted, Britain had not viewed it with favour. Although such a route would bring the Indian Ocean within easier reach of British shipping, so too would it facilitate the passage to the East for other powers. Furthermore, while de Lesseps was not an agent of the French Government, the French connection would surely increase the presence and influence of that nation in Egypt, and the France of Napoleon III – though briefly an ally in the Crimean War – was viewed with increasing distrust in Britain in the years immediately after that conflict. But by 1875 Napoleon had been crushed by Prussia and the Canal was now a fact, with four-fifths of its shipping sailing under the British flag. The improved facilities offered by the Canal for traffic with the East could not be ignored, susceptible though it was to financial and political manoeuvrings of the interested parties. When, therefore, the Khedive Ismail decided to sell his Canal shares Disraeli, the Prime Minister, seized the opportunity. The French were already in the market, but Disraeli raised the money quickly from the Rothschilds and within a fortnight of Ismail's intentions becoming known, the British Government acquired a controlling interest in the Suez Canal Company for £4 million.

Ismail's penury could not have come at a more fortuitous time for, with Russia now recovered from the stresses of the Crimean War, the Eastern Question re-awoke following the brutal suppression by the Turks of a rebellion among the Balkan Christians. In 1877 Russia declared war on the Sultan and her armies advanced into the Balkans. By early 1878, despite a bitter Turkish resistance, Russian troops were nearing Constantinople, the very threat which British foreign policy had for so long been designed to avoid. In Britain opinion was now grievously divided over that policy. To continue support for the Ottoman Empire was to condone Turkish atrocities in the Balkans, while to abandon the Turks would be handing Russia the keys to Constantinople, the Mediterranean and the Canal. In addition to this menace in the west, danger also loomed in the east where Russia, always ready to further her Mediterranean designs by capitalising on Britain's sensitivity over India, had been advancing her

Benjamin Disraeli, Earl of Beaconsfield. Twice Tory Prime Minister, in 1868 and from 1874–80, who gained for Britain a controlling interest in the Suez Canal. Painting dated 1881 by J.E. Millais.

Mohammed Tewfik, Khedive of Egypt 1879–92. Photograph *c* 1882.

frontiers in Central Asia and was again making overtures to Afghanistan.

In 1878 it looked as though Britain might have to go to war with Russia, and by the end of the year she was indeed in arms – but only against Afghanistan. Before that occurred, the danger in eastern Europe had been averted by the Congress of Berlin. By the earlier Treaty of San Stefano Russia had imposed upon the defeated Turks an independent Bulgaria which, being under Russian tutelage, would have afforded Russia access to the Aegean Sea. Such a strategic advantage could not be tolerated and at Berlin Disraeli, his diplomacy backed by the guns of a British fleet off the Dardanelles, secured a smaller Bulgaria and the retention of the Aegean coast in Turkish hands. In addition, to balance Russian annexations in Armenia and to provide a base for possible future aid to Turkey, the island of Cyprus was ceded by the Sultan to Britain. There were those in Britain, among them Sir Garnet Wolseley, appointed the first High Commissioner and Commander-in-Chief in Cyprus, who thought that Egypt would have served better, though after being in the island for a few months he came to the view that it would serve well enough as a place where a force could be concentrated for employment either in Asia Minor or Egypt. For the time being, with peace restored to the Balkans, Russian encroachments halted and any French monopoly of the Canal averted, Britain's artery to the East seemed safe enough.

In Egypt itself affairs were far from stable despite the £4 million paid over by Disraeli. The Rothschild money had provided only a temporary breathing space for Ismail whose foreign debt was of such staggering proportions – close on £81 million – that in 1876 he had to postpone payment of the interest on it. Egypt was finally bankrupt and with its European creditors baying for their money, there was nothing for it but for Ismail to accept foreign intervention in the form of an International Commission of Debt to put his finances in order. The powers most immediately concerned were Britain and France who imposed upon Ismail the services of two Controllers-General of Finance, one from each nation; the system of Dual Control as it was called. By 1878 control had begun to extend into government, with the Khedivial ministry supervised by British and French representatives who, though watchful of all measures taken by the new government, were equally watchful of each other, determined that neither country's influence should become predominant.

Britain's interests in Egypt were strategic and financial, both of which were threatened by a misgoverned and bankrupt Egypt. Possessed of a powerful Mediterranean fleet to check the expansionism of other powers in the area, she had no wish to annex or occupy Egypt with all the costs and risks of confrontation with other powers, particularly France, that such a course would entail. At the same time she was not prepared to allow France to convert her traditional interests in the country into an exclusive sphere of influence. Such an eventuality could be as injurious to the security of the Canal as instability in Egypt. For her part France had no desire to see the British Empire extending its domains into North Africa where her own Empire was then being established. It was in the interests of both powers that Egypt should be restored to solvency. For the time being, therefore, it was prudent that both should proceed in tandem.

At first the Khedive appeared to bow to the inevitable but soon, conscious of his loss of power and prestige, he began to strain against the bonds imposed upon him. He intrigued against the Dual Control, dismissed the British finance minister, appointed a purely Egyptian cabinet, and appealed to the nationalist and religious sensibilities of his Moslem subjects to throw off the foreign yoke. But his cry fell on deaf ears. His officials and officers were tired of their pay being in arrears and the fellahin, bled dry by Ismail's extravagance, had no cause or incentive to rise on his behalf. To the British and French it was clear they could expect no co-operation from Ismail, so in 1879 they persuaded his overlord, the Sultan of Turkey, to depose him and install in his place as Khedive his son Tewfik.

With the more malleable Tewfik on the throne, the scrutiny and control of Egyptian affairs became wider and more rigorous. However, it is often the case that medicine, no matter how beneficial, is unpalatable to the patient and can incur at best dislike and at worst distrust of the doctor, particularly if he is a stranger. So it was to be in Egypt. The people may not have had much for which to bless their Khedives but they *had* been their hereditary rulers, and masters in their own house however tyrannical their rule. Now they had a new ruler, albeit still hereditary, but one who was to seem, as time went by, no more than a puppet in the hands of foreigners, even though those foreigners were endeavouring to reform the system of tax collection that had borne so heavily upon the ordinary people. More equitable taxes, however, did not appeal to the upper classes who, having waxed fat and prospered in the days of Ismail, now apprehended a reduction of their wealth and power at the hands of these same foreigners. Religion too, so potent a force in Moslem countries, was degraded by the spectacle of power falling into the hands of the infidel. For Egypt to be made solvent, economies were essential in all Egyptian institutions, in all the trappings of a modernised state so enthusiastically built up by the House of Mahommed Ali. Among these was the Egyptian Army, not much of a force by European standards, but nevertheless, as in all despotisms, enjoying its own prestige and standing, from which accrued various perquisites to its senior officers. It was in the Army that the widening resentment of foreign intervention and a growing nationalist sentiment was to find expression; not among the senior officers, not among the rank and file but (as so often has been the case with military insurgency) in the middle ranks of the officer corps – in the person of Colonel Ahmed Arabi Bey.

2

Arabi's Revolt

The Egyptian Army in 1880 presented, in appearance, armaments and organisation, a very different aspect from the wild Oriental horde that had confronted Bonaparte at the turn of the century. With its Remington rifles and Krupp guns, its European and American advisors, its western-style uniforms (except for the ubiquitous red tarbush), it was essentially a modern force drawing its ethos from the Turkish service. Indeed many of its officers were Turks and Circassians, or from other Ottoman provinces, and the Sultan maintained titular control over it. However, the ranks of the Khedive's battalions were not filled by men of the same stamp as the stolid Anatolian infantry which had so stoutly resisted the Russians in 1877, nor even of the calibre of the ferocious Mameluke swordsmen of former times, but rather by the downtrodden, totally unwarlike fellahin from the villages of the Nile Delta. Torn from their families and fields by conscription and driven, sometimes in chains, to the barracks as their relations wept or wailed, convinced they would never be seen again, the fellahin had a terror of military service and many would resort to self-mutilation to avoid being taken. Once in the Army they were wretchedly paid – if paid at all – ill-fed and cheaply clothed, and were kept in ranks by the kourbash or, worst of all, the ever-present fear of being despatched to one of the distant garrisons of the Sudan, where interminable exile if not death awaited them. The European and American officers had little contact with the rank and file, being chiefly employed in technical and staff duties, while the Turks and Circassians filled the more senior ranks and were, in any case, contemptuous of the men under their command and indifferent to their welfare, being more interested in whatever personal benefits their rank and position could acquire for them.

The inadequacy and feeble morale of the Egyptian Army had been painfully revealed in 1876 when, in furtherance of the Khedive Ismail's expansionist ambitions in the region of the Upper Nile, a large force with an American Chief of Staff had been all but annihilated in Abyssinia. The survivors who returned to Egypt were bitter and disillusioned with the senior officers who had led them to disaster, and the cost of the expedition adversely affected the pay of both soldiers and junior officers. Most of the latter were drawn from the same Arabic-speaking fellah class as the men, and although their qualities or slightly superior status in village life had enabled them to gain commissions, their background, together with their distrust and resentment of their Turkish superiors – whose pay remained unaffected – led most of them to make common cause with the rank and file. Thus dissension grew within the Army. On the one hand were the Turkish and Circassian element, with pay and prospects unimpaired; on the other the native-born Egyptian junior ranks. When, a year or two later, financial economies led to the dismissal of 2500 officers, the ensuing disturbances among the fellah element resulted in the resignation of the Prime Minister, Nubar Pasha, and the English Finance Minister, Sir Rivers Wilson.

Prominent amid the growing unrest was a fellah officer who held the unusually high rank for one of his origins of lieutenant-colonel. This was Ahmed Arabi, the son of a small village

Types of the Egyptian Army, c 1882, in their blue (winter) and white (summer) uniforms. Top, from left: *1*) Lancer; *2*) Khedivial Guard; *3*) Officer in campaign dress; *4*) Circassian. Centre: *5*) Gendarme; *6*) Berber, Bedouin, Albanian and Circassian irregulars; *7*) Black (Sudanese) Regiment of the Guard. Bottom: *8*) Infantry officer; *9*) Guard horse artillery; *10*) Mounted Gendarme; *11*) Infantrymen.

MONTBARD.

Krupp field gun as used by the Egyptian artillery.

sheikh, who had been born in 1840 and received some education as a boy at the Azhar University in Cairo. Being tall and well-built for his age, he had been conscripted into the Army when he was only fourteen. At first employed as a clerk he attracted the attention of his superiors and by the age of seventeen had been made an officer, following the introduction of a scheme of the then Viceroy, Said, who being well-intentioned towards the fellahin, wished to increase the number of fellah officers. Arabi's imposing figure and presence won him the personal favour of the Viceroy, which secured for him the appointment of Viceregal ADC, plus his advancement from the rank of lieutenant to lieutenant-colonel within the space of only three years. Such rapid promotion was too good to last and, after his benefactor Said's death, he fell into disfavour under Ismail, in whose spectacular schemes there was no place for lowly-born fellah officers. The contrast between Said's benevolent interest in the fellahin and Ismail's tyranny and contempt, together with the stagna-

tion of his own career, bred in Arabi not only discontent with his own lot but also a growing desire to right the wrongs done to the class from which he had sprung, the indigenous population of Egypt. By the time of the Abyssinian campaign he still held the rank he had so speedily achieved sixteen years before, and although he was only employed in safety on the lines of communication, the fiasco that befell the Army drove him deeper into intrigues against the Khedive and the Turco-Circassian ruling class. Any plan that Arabi and his adherents may have conceived to get rid of Ismail proved unnecessary in the event as the work was done for them by the Dual Control, and the accession of Tewfik was welcomed by Arabi and by the liberal, religious reform movement then active at the Azhar University.

By the autumn of 1880 Egypt, under its new Khedive and guided by the Dual Control, seemed to be turning a corner. The finances and administration were being put in order and the wretched lot of the fellahin was being improved, though of course an enormous amount remained to be done. Fortune again smiled on Arabi personally, for Tewfik appointed him colonel of one of the Guard regiments quartered in Cairo. Nevertheless all was not as well as it seemed and the chief source of trouble lay in the lingering discontent in the Army. This was exacerbated by the appointment as Minister for War of Osman Rifki Pasha, a Turk with all the prejudices of his class against the fellahin. As the fellah officers saw it, it was they who were dismissed with pay and pensions cut back or withheld when economies were being made, their soldiers who were employed as cheap labour on menial non-military tasks, while the Circassians were favoured and promoted. These grievances, which were not without substance, found a spokesman in Arabi who, with other fellah officers, petitioned the War Ministry for an enquiry. Such a step was perfectly justifiable but then, conscious that their action would earn them the hostility of Osman Rifki, Arabi and two other colonels of the Cairo regiments thought to protect themselves by making a direct appeal to the Prime Minister, Riaz Pasha, for the removal of the War Minister. Riaz viewed this as insubordination but undertook to look into the colonels' complaints. When he later suggested to Arabi that his action could be construed as disloyalty to the Khedive, Arabi agreed to leave the matter in the hands of Osman Rifki.

On 1 February 1881 the three colonels were summoned by the War Minister to the Kasr-el-Nil Barracks, ostensibly to arrange the military ceremonial for the wedding of a Royal princess. Once there, they were arrested and cross-examined, but help was soon at hand. For Arabi and his friends, having had foreknowledge of the plot against them, had arranged that their regiments should march to the rescue if they did not emerge from Kasr-el-Nil within two hours. As the investigation continued, Arabi's troops suddenly burst in, overturning the tables and chairs, pelting the senior officers with inkpots and chasing Osman Rifki out of a window. Full of euphoria at the comic scene they had created, the troops, headed by their band and their three colonels, marched off to the Abdin Palace where the colonels summoned the Khedive to appear and demanded the dismissal of the War Minister. Without any loyal troops at his back, Tewfik yielded. Out went Osman Rifki and in his place was appointed Mahmud Sami, one of the Turkish ruling class but a man with ambitions of his own where the future government of Egypt was concerned, who saw in Arabi a useful tool in the advancement of himself. Having achieved their aim in this high-handed fashion, the colonels were somewhat subdued by what they had done and hastened to pledge their allegiance to the Khedive, apologising for the disturbance they had caused.

Although the fellah element of the Army had now demonstrated (for the second time) its power to act against the ruling Turco-Circassians, and the authority of the Khedive as absolute monarch had been shown to be hollow, such were the intrigues and distrust that permeated governmental circles that Arabi and his confederates did not rest easy. For a while things quietened down, 'as though everybody concerned was somewhat alarmed at what he had done or allowed to be done and only desired to be quiet and not talked about', as Sir

Colonel Ahmed Arabi Bey, 1839–1911. Engraving from a photograph c 1882.

Edward Malet, the British Agent and Consul-General put it.

Malet's view of the colonels' action was that it was purely an expression of dissent within the Egyptian Army, with which he was not without sympathy, and though it had shown up the weakness of the Khedive, it was not directed against or inspired by hostile feelings towards the Dual Control. 'But,' he wrote, 'tomorrow? Suppose the troops next ask for the dismissal of the whole Ministry or of the European control?' Since Malet's appointment in 1879, a Liberal Government under Gladstone had taken office but had accepted the former administration's policy of joint action with France in Egyptian affairs to restore stability and prosperity to the country. Malet had always endeavoured to act in concert with his French opposite number, but after the incident of 1 February it transpired

William Ewart Gladstone. Four times Liberal Prime Minister, including the period 1880–85. Painting dated 1879 by J.E. Millais.

intending to occupy Egypt, in the same way as France, at that time, was taking over Tunis; a country, like Egypt, within the dominion of the Ottoman Empire, which had already protested to France against its action. To allay such fears, which were quite without foundation, Malet planned a visit to the Sublime Porte to show that Britain and the Sultan were in accord over Egypt, a step which he also hoped might deter the colonels from further insurrection for fear of retribution from the Porte.

At the very time he was in Constantinople awaiting an audience with the Sultan, he heard that his February misgivings (about the Cairo military again showing their strength) had been realised. On 9 September, Arabi and his fellow colonels had marched their regiments to the Abdin Palace and confronted the Khedive with demands for the dismissal of his entire Ministry, the convocation of a National Parliament, and the increase of the Army to 18,000 men. This was no mere remonstrance about military injustice but a deliberate challenge, backed by force, to the Khedivial authority.

Ever since Arabi's action in February, his reputation as the champion of the native-born Egyptians against the Turco-Circassian masters had been increasing among both the ordinary people and the liberal reform movement, so that he had become a prominent figure. At the same time he feared the vengeance of the Khedive and Riaz Pasha, although he was confident he would receive due warning from the War Minister. Then, in August, Mahmud Sami was dismissed and replaced by the Khedive's brother-in-law, Daoud Pasha, who was given the brief of stamping out insubordination in the Army. Arabi and his friends at once feared for their safety and when Daoud decided to disperse the Cairo regiments, they acted. Confronted by Arabi's bayonets the Khedive again yielded. A new Government took office under Sherif Pasha, a man of liberal views, and Mahmud Sami was reinstated as War Minister at the insistence of the colonels. The question of a constitution and the increase to the Army were to be considered, although Malet had discovered that the former would never be

that the latter had been in communication – if not collusion – with the colonels. As a result of representations made by the Khedive to the French Government, the French Agent was recalled so that, for a while, the parity of influence between France and Britain over the Egyptian Government was lost. While Malet did all he could to restore confidence between the Khedive and the military party, with the ultimate view of establishing a constitutional system in Egypt, he became aware of a growing suspicion within the country that Britain was

THEATRE OF OPERATIONS IN EGYPT, 1882

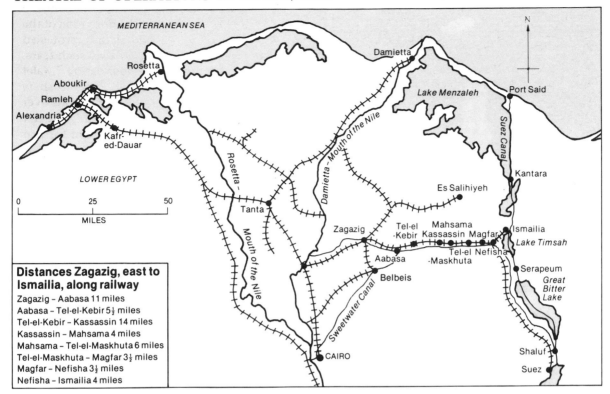

MEDITERRANEAN SEA

Rosetta
Aboukir
Ramleh
Alexandria
Kafr-ed-Dauar

LOWER EGYPT

Damietta
Lake Menzaleh
Port Said
Suez Canal
Kantara
Es Salihiyeh
Ismailia
Lake Timsah
Serapeum
Great Bitter Lake
Shaluf
Suez

Tanta
Zagazig
Tel-el-Kebir
Mahsama
Kassassin Magfar
Tel-el Nefisha
Aabasa
Tel-el-Maskhuta
Belbeis
CAIRO

Rosetta - Mouth of the Nile
Damietta - Mouth of the Nile
Mouth of the Nile
Sweetwater Canal

0   25   50
MILES

Distances Zagazig, east to Ismailia, along railway

Zagazig – Aabasa 11 miles
Aabasa – Tel-el-Kebir 5½ miles
Tel-el-Kebir – Kassassin 14 miles
Kassassin – Mahsama 4 miles
Mahsama – Tel-el-Maskhuta 6 miles
Tel-el-Maskhuta – Magfar 3½ miles
Magfar – Nefisha 3½ miles
Nefisha – Ismailia 4 miles

countenanced by the Sultan, while the latter, because of the expense involved, would be subject to the scrutiny of the Franco-British controllers of the national finances. As a first step towards a more constitutional form of government, a Chamber of Notables was approved and a compromise over the money demanded for the Army was in due course arrived at.

After this Arabi's prestige and the spirit of nationalism increased throughout the country. In this new climate the attitude towards the European control varied.

The more realistic appreciated that their liberation from Ismail's profligacy was due to the foreigners, that foreign expertise was still necessary, and that the implementation of a Constitution, in the face of the Sultan's objections, would require foreign intercession. On the other hand, there was a desire abroad to be rid of foreign control, and a distrust of Britain's and France's motives lingered on. While remaining wary of the Egyptian military, the British Government was not averse to a gradual

progression towards a constitutional system, and in an effort to calm Egyptian suspicions a statement was issued in November by the Foreign Secretary, Lord Granville, which clearly emphasised that his Government's policy had 'no other aim than the prosperity of the country and its full enjoyment of that liberty which it has obtained from the Sultan'.

Any good that this statement, and the assembly of the Chamber of Notables in December, may have done to increase confidence and stability was abruptly undone soon afterwards. The new French Prime Minister, Gambetta, took a far less sanguine view of Egyptian nationalism than Britain, seeing in it an incitement to disaffection in the French North African Empire and a bulwark against the spread of French influence in Egypt. He proposed to Britain that both Governments should strengthen the Khedive's position by the issue of a Joint Note, stressing their agreed determination to maintain the Khedive on the throne 'as alone able to guarantee the good

A warship of Admiral Sir Beauchamp Seymour's Alexandria squadron, the ironclad HMS *Alexandra*, completed 1877. One of this ship's company, Gunner Harding, won the Victoria Cross at Alexandria for disposing of an unexploded Egyptian shell.

order and the development of general prosperity in Egypt', to which end they would oppose together all internal and external dangers which might threaten the Khedive and 'the order of things established in Egypt'. The British Government was not entirely happy, but deeming it important to remain on good terms with France and maintain parity of influence and believing that if read in conjunction with its own November statement the Note would be acceptable, the text was agreed after inserting a reservation that it did not commit the Government to any particular mode of action. On 8 January 1882 the Note was published in Egypt.

Its effect was catastrophic. It frightened the Khedive, it enraged the Nationalists with its implied menace to the reforms achieved, drove the more moderate elements to side with the militants, and incensed all, including the Turco-Circassians, by its threat of foreign inter-

vention. Arabi, who was now Under Secretary for War, was furious, claiming that a joint Franco-British policy meant that, as France had taken Tunis, so would Britain take Egypt. From henceforth the nationalist movement became more and more directed against the Dual Control, seeking everywhere to oust the European officials. Since the Khedive was now firmly linked, in the nationalist view, with the Franco-British representatives, respect for his authority diminished while Arabi's increased. By February, after a clash between the Chamber of Notables and the foreign Controllers-General over the budget, a new Government took office with Mahmud Sami as Prime Minister and Arabi as War Minister. In April Sir Edward Malet wrote, 'Militarism is increasing in every direction and the country will soon be governed by nothing but officers.'

With the Army wholly under his control, ultimate power within Egypt lay in Arabi's hands. The measures he took to increase its size, and to improve the pay and promotion prospects of officers favourable to him, alerted the financial controllers and incurred the enmity of Circassian officers who had been passed over.

An alleged conspiracy against Arabi's life by some of the latter led to their arrest, a secret court-martial without defence facilities for the accused, and a sentence of banishment to a remote part of the Sudan, which was tantamount to death. The Khedive's refusal to confirm the sentence propelled him into an outright conflict of wills with Arabi, in the course of which public order in the country began to be threatened and the safety of the 90,000 European population endangered. The Khedive, with nothing to buttress his authority but the support of the British and French governments, stood firm but his refusal to yield increased his isolation and the anti-European feeling. After a request for intervention to the Sultan had met with little but prevarication, Britain and France decided to send a joint naval squadron to Alexandria in earnest of their support for the Khedive and to protect Europeans. At the same time Arabi was warned that he would be held responsible for any outbreak of serious trouble, but that if he was loyal to the Khedive no action would be taken against him.

With the arrival of the Allied warships on 20 May, some of Arabi's non-military adherents wavered but the military party remained intransigent, warning that France and Britain intended the disbandment of the Army, the banishment of officers and the occupation of Egypt with troops. It was clear that no Ministry containing Arabi could be counted as loyal to the Khedive and on 25 May the British and French agents required the dismissal of Arabi and two of his fellow colonels. The Khedive acquiesced, and the entire Ministry resigned accusing him of bowing to a degree of foreign interference which outreached that agreed at his accession.

To get rid of a disloyal government was one thing, to form a loyal one was a different matter, particularly as the Army was now in open defiance with Arabi demanding the deposition of the Khedive, if not his death, unless he were reinstated as War Minister. At first the Khedive refused, but when Arabi compelled, under pain of death, some religious leaders to intercede on his behalf, the Khedive, a prisoner in his own palace with his life at risk, had no alternative but to agree.

HMS *Inflexible*, sister ship of *Invincible*, Seymour's flagship, mounting four 80-ton guns in two turrets, one of which is visible on the port side between the two funnels. This ironclad was only completed the year before Seymour's bombardment of Alexandria.

The Khedive's authority had now totally lost all credibility. The people saw in Arabi's triumph the imminent expulsion of all foreigners and Christians with the result that religious hysteria mounted and outrages started to occur against the Christian community. All governmental work was at a standstill except at the War Ministry and panic, bred of disorder, manifested itself in Cairo and Alexandria. At the latter, troops began to construct batteries and earthworks abreast of the allied warships.

In the midst of all this rising tension the ponderous deliberations of the Sublime Porte, to whom numerous appeals had been made, at last bore fruit with the arrival on 7 June of a Turkish Commissioner, Dervish Pasha, who assured the Khedive that he had come to restore Khedivial authority. At first it appeared he would take a firm line with the military party, though the latter showed no sign of coming to heel, but before anything concrete could be achieved, the pent-up excitement exploded into violence.

Alexandria at this time was a highly cosmopolitan city, its inhabitants including all the races of the Levant, Christian and Moslem, Europeans, Africans and Indians. It was also a city of contrasts between wealth and poverty: on the one hand the teeming bazaars and narrow alleys, on the other the splendid, modern, European buildings. 'Everything which tends to promote racial hatred and national instability was here to be discerned.' On the afternoon of 11 June a riot broke out between Moslems and Christians. Somewhat belatedly Arabi ordered out troops to restore order but not before fifty Europeans had been killed with many others, including the British Consul, injured, as well as an uncertain number of Moslems. It was thought that the seamen and marines aboard the warships were too few in number to land to protect the European community, and in any case such a step was likely to provoke more trouble. The city quietened down the next day, but more and more Europeans began leaving, not only in Alexandria but throughout the country, with consequent closing down of businesses and the indigenous employees being left without work. The public services, too, were affected.

Dervish Pasha was unable to make much headway in his mission, though he did succeed in bringing the Khedive from Cairo to greater safety at Alexandria where the fleet was at hand. Everywhere fear and unrest grew, with the military of all ranks adopting an arrogant and overbearing attitude. The construction of seaward fortifications at Alexandria continued unabated, causing concern to the British Admiral, Sir Beauchamp Seymour, while the presence of threatening Arab bands along the Canal gave rise to fears for its safety.

In Britain the state of Egyptian affairs had been overshadowed in Gladstone's mind by the Irish question. The Government's policy had been to act diplomatically in concert with the French in the Khedive's support, putting its trust in the Sultan to provide military intervention, should this become necessary to restore order, although the French were opposed to the use of Turkish troops. Any use of British troops, alone or jointly with France, was to be avoided at all costs. However, the Alexandria riots forced Gladstone to concentrate on the Egyptian crisis, for he was now faced with pressure from the Whig and Radical elements in his Cabinet to intervene. Though violently opposed to the use of military means, Gladstone could not afford any disunity in his Cabinet which might imperil his measures for Ireland. On 15 June, the Cabinet considered for the first time the propriety of making preparations for the possible contingency of British military intervention. The next day the Secretary for War, Hugh Childers, discussed in greatest secrecy what would need to be done with the Commander-in-Chief, the Duke of Cambridge, and the Adjutant-General, Sir Garnet Wolseley.

On 23 June a conference of the European Powers assembled at Constantinople to consider what could be done to induce Turkey to intervene in Egypt. Since the Porte at first declined to be represented little could be achieved. In any case, the very next day the hands of Britain and France were forced further by the exclusion of their Controllers-General from a sitting of the Nationalist Ministry in Cairo, while Arabi announced that any military intervention would be resisted with force.

Although in Britain the Cabinet was still reluctant to use troops, the military planning went ahead. On 3 July Wolseley produced an outline plan for the employment of two infantry divisions and a cavalry brigade for the seizure of the Canal and a subsequent advance on Cairo. The administrative arrangements for the transport and maintenance of such a force were fully worked out and on the next day secret warning orders were issued to the com-

1st Battalion Scots Guards disembarking at Alexandria on 12 August 1882: almost one month to the day after the Royal Navy's bombardment of the city.

manding officers of the units earmarked. The Government still hoped that, if it came to intervention, this might be limited to the protection of the Canal and, as a precautionary measure, two battalions and a company of engineers were ordered from Malta to Cyprus under Major-General Alison, ready to act in conjunction with the Royal Navy. This force left Malta on 8 July.

Meanwhile at Alexandria the strengthening of the Egyptian defences went on despite the representations of Admiral Seymour. The forts, which in all mounted some 180 guns, extended for about four and a half miles, from the Pharos just north of the city, round the harbour and along the shore to Fort Marabout in the south-west, with the powerful Fort Meks and its thirty-one guns midway between the two extremities. At one time it seemed that the Egyptians had agreed to cease work but the ships' searchlights revealed that their efforts were continued at night. Concerned for the safety of his ships and crews, and furious with the duplicity of the Egyptians, Seymour issued an ultimatum on 10 July on his own authority

that, unless the forts were surrendered to him within 24 hours, he would open fire. That evening the French warships sailed away for Port Said. At seven o'clock next morning, no word having come from Arabi, the bombardment began.

The Royal Navy's ships had undergone greater changes in the two decades that had ensued since 1860 than had occurred in the three centuries prior to that date. At the time of the Crimean War the fleet had largely consisted of wooden sailing ships little different in appearance from those of Nelson's day, though many had auxiliary steam engines driving screw propellers. Ten years later the Navy had thirty 'ironclads', still rigged for sail but with hulls of wrought-iron which was made thicker as guns became more powerful. Unlike the old wooden ships firing broadsides from two or three gundecks, the new ironclads were designed to provide fire ahead and astern as well as broadside.

One of the Egyptian shore batteries after Seymour's bombardment.

HMS *Alexandra*, launched in 1877 and one of Seymour's ships, mounted two 11-inch and ten 10-inch guns capable of piercing $13\frac{1}{2}$ and 12 inches of wrought-iron respectively and arranged on two decks so that four guns could fire ahead or six broadside; her armour plating was 12 inches thick round the waterline and 8–10 inches round the battery. These guns, muzzle-loading but with rifled barrels and enormously thick in the breech, were fired through gunports as on the old wooden men-of-war, and were mounted on heavy iron carriages which could be traversed by means of a brass rail laid in an arc on the deck. *Alexandra's* guns weighed around 25 tons but the most up-to-date of Seymour's battleships, HMS *Invincible* (the flagship) and *Inflexible* each had four 80-ton guns, mounted in pairs in two turrets positioned to fire ahead and astern at diagonally opposite corners of a central, armoured citadel occupying a third of the length of the ship. Such ships were still rigged for sail though on a reduced scale with only two masts, but their propulsion depended chiefly on the efforts of 120 stokers, far below deck, wheeling the coal from bunkers to the stokeholes at either end of the engine rooms. If the heat of the Mediterranean sun in mid-July blazing down on iron-built ships was exhausting for the gun crews, for the stokers the conditions must have been suffocating.

Throughout the morning Seymour's eight battleships and eleven gunboats kept up the thunderous bombardment. So thick was the smoke emitted from the great guns that officers had to climb aloft to direct the fire, though their corrections frequently went unheard in the din. The huge guns of *Inflexible* and *Invincible* took so long to load that they could only be fired every five minutes, while on other ships the gun-layers, trained to allow for the roll of the vessel, experienced difficulty in adjusting to a flat, calm sea and frequently had to readjust their aim following the massive discharge and recoil of the guns on either side.

Royal Naval landing parties with 9-pounder guns from Seymour's squadron ashore in Egypt. The officers are wearing helmets, the ratings Sennet straws.

Nevertheless it was an uneven contest, for although the Egyptian artillerymen fought their guns bravely, scoring a number of hits particularly against HMS *Sultan* and *Alexandra*, their fire on the whole was poorly directed and failed to incapacitate any of the ships or inflict serious casualties. Egyptian losses, on the other hand, were heavy and by 4.30 in the afternoon the forts had been silenced. Observing each phase of the bombardment from *Invincible* was a tall, striking young subaltern of the Royal Engineers with an imposing moustache, supposedly on sick leave from his survey work in Cyprus. A week before he and another officer had gone ashore disguised as Levantines to spy out Arabi's defences and dispositions. This was his first experience of action in the lands of the Nile but it would by no means be his last. His name was Horatio Herbert Kitchener.

On the following day Arabi evacuated his troops and withdrew inland, leaving Alexandria in flames while mobs roamed the streets looting and wreaking their vengeance on any Europeans they could find. Throughout that day and into the next, riot and conflagration reigned and it was not until 14 July that Seymour landed a force of seamen and marines to fight the fires and restore order.

Meanwhile General Alison in Cyprus, unaware of the cause of these events and out of communications, believed that the military expedition, of which his force was to be the advanced guard, must now be under way, and therefore sailed for Port Said ready to carry out his ordained task of seizing the Canal. On arrival he learned the true facts and, realising the need for troops to restore order at Alexandria, he sailed on there, disembarking his men, of the 1st South Staffordshire and 3rd King's Royal Rifle Corps, on 17 May thus allowing the exhausted naval landing parties to be relieved. The Khedive, who throughout this period had been at his palace at Ramleh some four miles up the coast and in considerable danger from

35

Arabi's men, was moved into the Ras-el-Tin Palace in Alexandria itself where he could be better protected. When order was restored, Alison began to prepare a defensive position in case of attack by Arabi, who was constructing strong entrenchments at Kafr-ed-Dauar, only 14 miles south-east down the Alexandria-Cairo railway. By 29 July, after receiving further reinforcements, Alison, whose operation had begun purely as a policing task in the ravaged city, had established a firm bridgehead around Alexandria and Ramleh, with his positions connected by a railway and his exposed right flank protected by an armoured train mounting guns and machine-guns manned by sailors. Two days earlier the House of Commons had voted a credit of £2,300,000 and the die was cast for a British expedition.

Since Seymour's bombardment on 11 July this had become almost inevitable, as the

NCOs and men of 3rd Battalion, King's Royal Rifle Corps, one of the first two battalions to be landed at Alexandria in July 1882. The Sergeant-Major sits in the centre with, on his right, the Quartermaster-Sergeant, a pioneer and a bugler. The uniforms are rifle-green with red piping, the equipment is black.

The armoured train manned by the Royal Navy which formed part of General Alison's defences at Alexandria.

Egyptain Nationalists were now inflamed to a new pitch. The Khedive had again formally dismissed Arabi on the 16th but, with his authority now in tatters, he found himself denounced in turn by Arabi, who was appointed Commander-in-Chief by a military committee selected from the Chamber of Notables. Henceforth Arabi was the effective ruler of Egypt. At Constantinople the Powers' efforts to get the Sultan to commit troops in support of the lawful Khedive met with the usual procrastination. When on 19 July it was learned that the Porte would do no more than send a delegate to the Conference, it was clear that Britain and France would have to act. Gladstone and his Foreign Secretary still hoped that an occupation of the Canal with a small force would suffice, but they were under pressure from Lord Hartington, the Secretary for India, Joseph Chamberlain and Hugh Childers, all of whom were convinced that only a large, well-found expedition with Cairo as the final objective could overthrow Arabi, restore the Khedive and maintain the security of the Canal. On 20 July, Gladstone reluctantly agreed. It was soon evident that it was to be a unilateral undertaking: France, having at first refused to consider more than the protection of the Canal, took fright at what Germany might do while her back was turned in Egypt and bilked at the whole idea of intervention, thus losing all chance of establishing that sphere of influence on which she had set so much store. None of the other Powers were prepared to act and the Sultan preferred to avoid the issue. On seeking the vote of credit Gladstone stressed that intervention was merely a short-term operation in the name of the Khedive to save Egypt from anarchy and restore the rule of law. Such sentiments were, of course, balm to the Liberal conscience. But in reality British troops were going to Egypt, not out of concern for Tewfik and the Egyptians, but to safeguard British interests: for as Lord Granville had pointed out on 11 July in a despatch to Constantinople, not only was much British capital invested in the country, but Egypt was situated 'on the most direct maritime route between England and her Indian possessions and Australian colonies.' It was now up to Wolseley and the recently reorganised Army, supported by the Navy, to ensure that the vital route did not fall into hostile hands.

3

Britain Makes Ready

The British Army which was about to launch an expeditionary force on to Egyptian soil had just emerged from a series of modernising reforms that had first begun after the Crimean War, but which had gathered momentum under a Liberal Secretary of State for War, Edward Cardwell, and had recently been completed by another Liberal, Hugh Childers, who had taken office in 1880. The post-Crimean reforms had made Parliamentary control over the Army more efficient, by centralising its administration within the War Office instead of its being spread over various departments as hitherto; they had improved the soldiers' clothing and weapons, and established the Staff College for the training of suitable officers, and other schools of instruction; and had begun to reorganise the fighting Arms' logistic support — an area which had proved so defective in the Crimea — by removing its functions from civilian or regimental control and handing them over to specialised corps, from which have developed what are known today as the 'Services' — Royal Army Medical Corps, Royal Army Ordinance Corps and so on. These innovations, particularly the last, were not to be completed until the end of the century, but by the time of the Egyptian campaign they were well under way.

On taking office in 1868 Cardwell inherited an Army in which officers of cavalry and infantry, though not of artillery and engineers, obtained their commissions and much of their subsequent promotion by purchase. Within three years Cardwell had abolished purchase, all officers in future gaining their commissions after training at Sandhurst for cavalry and infantry and Woolwich for artillery and engineers. Promotion thereafter was to be by seniority tempered by selection, and controlled by compulsory retirement at certain ages, and

limitations on the tenure of regimental and battalion command. The recruitment of soldiers and manning of the Army had depended on voluntary enlistment for long service. This system had served well enough in the period between the Napoleonic and Crimean Wars, when the Army's task had been the garrisoning of Ireland, India and a few other colonies. The Crimean War, followed quickly by the Indian Mutiny and increased Imperial commitments, had revealed that the system was under strain. Furthermore, the doubtful intentions of Napoleon III, the rising power of Prussia and the expansionism of Russia made it plain that the Army's role was no longer merely Imperial but European as well, ready to defend the home base and, if need be, deploy an expeditionary force overseas. With a small, long-service Army there were no reserves of trained men who could be recalled to the Colours in the event of a sudden need to expand the forces available. There was, to be sure, the Militia, 80,000 strong (at least on paper), and the Volunteers, raised for home defence only, but the former suffered from neglect and lack of training and the latter were conspicuous more for their enthusiasm than for their efficiency. In no way could the British Army mobilise a field force of 400,000 men in short order, as Prussia had done against Austria in 1866. In any case, in an age of growing prosperity and increasing emigration, voluntary enlistment for long service was no longer as fruitful as in the past.

Prussia and other European powers relied upon conscription for short service, followed by a period on the reserve; but conscription in Britain was politically unthinkable and the constant turnover of men would not serve for the Imperial role. In 1871, therefore, Cardwell abolished long service in favour of a twelve-year engagement, of which six years would be

Detachment of one of the Army's specialised corps, formed since 1856, the Army Hospital Corps, as equipped for the Egyptian expedition. The uniform is blue with cherry-red piping. Attached to the helmets are specially-issued goggles and anti-fly veils. The AHC was subsequently incorporated in the Royal Army Medical Corps.

served with the Colours and the balance with the reserve. By this means a reserve of trained men would be built up and, allied with improved pay and living conditions, would – it was hoped – attract a better type of man into the ranks. Impressed by the localised organisation of the Prussian Army, Cardwell decided to apply it to the Infantry of the Line, which hitherto consisted of a series of quite independent numbered regiments, some with two battalions but the majority with only one, each with its own depot company for recruitment, training and drafting to the parent battalion. Although most regiments had held some subsidiary territorial title since 1782, these had no practical significance, either as recruiting areas or locations for the depots. In contrast, the Militia and Volunteer battalions were all localised. In 1872–1873 Cardwell introduced his localisation scheme whereby two regular regiments, though retaining their separate identities, were linked for mutual support, with Militia and Volunteer battalions affiliated to them, all based on one district and with a common depot located in the district. Not only did Cardwell hope that such a scheme would stimulate recruiting through local pride but that, by equalising the number of Line battalions between home and abroad, no two regular battalions of a district would be overseas at the same time, thus easing the manning problem.

Things did not work out quite as Cardwell had intended. Leaving aside the Army's innate

Field-Marshal HRH the Duke of Cambridge, Commander-in-Chief of the British Army from 1856–95.

example of how wrong the system could go, both battalions of the 24th Regiment found themselves in the Zulu War and when the 1st Battalion was decimated at Isandhlwana, there was no home battalion to replenish its ranks with trained men, only newly-enlisted recruits in the depot or volunteers from home battalions in other districts.

When Childers took office in 1880, he increased the soldier's active engagement to seven years with the Colours, and eight for India and the Colonies. To overcome criticisms about the 'mere boys' enlisted under short service, he raised the minimum age for enlistment from eighteen to nineteen and stipulated that no man was to go to India until he was twenty. The pay and promotion prospects of non-commissioned officers were improved by the introduction of warrant rank, and by allowing all corporals to remain on the active list for twelve years or re-engage for twenty-one, and all sergeants for twenty-one years, subject to certain provisos. He next tackled the unpopularity of the linked-regiments system, not by unlinking them as some urged, but by carrying Cardwell's scheme to its logical and even more unpopular conclusion: the conversion of the regimental district into a territorial regiment of two regular battalions and a number of Militia and Volunteer battalions, all with the same title derived from the county or district, the same uniform and badges. For the senior, low-numbered regiments which already had two regular battalions, this revolutionary departure from past practice was less abhorrent than for the remainder. Each of these found itself inextricably joined to another, losing in the process its treasured number and identity, and acquiring instead a sometimes hated or despised partner as its sister battalion to which at any time its members might be transferred, and the title of a county to which they might not feel the slightest affinity. Childers' scheme, effective from 1 July 1881, though logical and sensible, was

conservatism, and notwithstanding the build-up of the reserves and the generally beneficial effect of short service on the calibre of recruits, the numbers enlisted did not compensate for the higher turnover of men actually with the Colours. Consequently many a home battalion of a district had to be whittled away in strength to keep the foreign battalion fully manned. The linking of regiments was unpopular, being seen as a threat to the individuality of each regiment, while identification with a geographical area proved no substitute for the traditional loyalty to a particular regiment as epitomised in its time-honoured numeral. Furthermore, due to increased commitments abroad – three campaigns occurring between 1878 and 1881 – the equalisation of battalions between home and abroad proved impossible to achieve. As an

Lieutenant-General Sir Garnet Wolseley in 1880 when holding the appointment of Quartermaster-General. Painting by A. Besnard.

Officers and men of 1st Battalion South Staffordshire Regiment in camp at Ramleh. The officer in the Glengarry is Major Sir Norman Pringle Bt. This battalion landed with the 3rd/60th Rifles at Alexandria in July 1882. The uniform is scarlet serge frocks with white collars and blue trousers. The white foreign service helmets have been stained.

Opposite below: Lieutenant-Colonel Hon.O.G.P.Montague and officers of the Royal Horse Guards (The Blues) squadron of the composite Household Cavalry Regiment formed for the Egyptian expedition.

Below: Major-General Sir Archibald Alison (centre seated) and staff. He commanded the British troops at Alexandria until Wolseley's arrival and later took over the Highland Brigade. He lost his left arm at Lucknow in the Indian Mutiny.

greeted with dismay and anger, and indeed it would take nearly forty years until the regiments, welded together by the fires of the Great War, generally accepted it. The Egyptian campaign of 1882 was the first in which infantry battalions fought under their new designations, but so unfamiliar were these, that they continued to be described by their old numerals: for example, the 1st South Staffords, who have already been met at Alexandria, were still customarily called the 38th.

For all its advantages the new scheme failed to overcome the imbalance between home and abroad, nor did it solve the problem of keeping the home battalions up to strength and fit for war, in particular for a sudden requirement for an expeditionary force as occurred in the middle of 1882. The reserves built up by the short service system were intended for the expansion of the Army in what Childers called 'a great national emergency', not for 'a small war'. He had plans in train for an overall increase in Infantry strength of 3000, by which he hoped to build up sixteen battalions at home and eight in the Mediterranean, each not less than 800 strong. However, when it was decided to send a force to Egypt in July these plans were insufficiently far advanced and the designated units had to be reinforced by calling out reservists who had left the Colours in the previous two years.

The opposition to all these reforms found its

A private of the 1st Life Guards in his Egyptian service dress. Watercolour by R. Simkin.

their efforts to reduce his prestige – had convinced him that the post-1870 reforms were too quick, too many and too drastic. The very things that Cardwell and Childers saw as vital for the modernisation and efficiency of the Army, Cambridge saw as destructive of all that was best in it. In his struggles to resist the abolition of purchase, to retain long service (which alone could provide seasoned soldiers) and to preserve regimental *esprit de corps*, he had much support from the Queen and elements within the Army.

There were also in the Army those who took a contrary view and put all their weight behind the reforms, men who felt as strongly about the service in their way as Cambridge did in his. Foremost among these was Garnet Wolseley, ambitious, impatient, snobbish, clever and as contemptuous of politicians as was the Duke, a man who had made a considerable reputation for himself in colonial campaigns since 1870. After arriving too late in South Africa to retrieve the early disasters of the Zulu War, he failed to get the chief command in India in 1880 owing to objections by Cambridge. In 1881 the Duke threatened resignation when Childers appointed Wolseley to the second post in the Army, that of Adjutant-General, a position that would inevitably bring him into the closest contact with the Commander-in-Chief. Since the latter regarded Wolseley as 'underhand, untrue, false, disloyal, overbearing and bumptious to a degree', and Wolseley felt his superior to be 'an old obstacle to all progress' and 'a bow-and-arrow general', such a partnership was unlikely to be a happy or fruitful one. The row over Wolseley's appointment had to be smoothed down by the Queen's intervention, but the two men, 'professionally as far as possible divergent', would have to endure each other for fourteen years.

In 1882 Wolseley was at the height of his powers and it was under his energetic guidance that the contingency planning for the Egyptian expedition, both as to the administrative measures and the outline of operations, went ahead. It was a mark of his prescience that his memorandum of 3 July pinpointed the very place where the decisive action of such a cam-

chief champion in the holder of a high office which, as it happened, Childers was then endeavouring to subordinate to the authority of the War Secretary (as Cardwell had in his time), to buttress Parliamentary control. The office was that of Commander-in-Chief, located at the Horse Guards, and had been held since 1856 by the Queen's cousin, the Duke of Cambridge, appointed at the early age of 37 after respectable but unremarkable service in the Crimean War. Conscientious, hard-working and motivated by a sincere love for the Army, Cambridge had shown himself in his early years in office as receptive to progress, but increasing age – allied to a deep distrust of politicians, particularly of the Liberal persuasion, and a resentment of paign was likely to be fought. However much Cambridge may have been exasperated by Wolseley and what was being done to the Army, he was realistic enough to recognise the latter's ability and intelligence, not to mention their common dislike of politicians, so there were no Royal objections to the Government's proposal of giving Wolseley command of the force.

Both the Duke and Wolseley were in agreement that Gladstone's hopes of confining military operations to a seizure of the Canal by

Privates and drummers of the Coldstream Guards in home and foreign service marching order. The difference between the home service tunic and the scarlet serge frock as worn in Egypt can be clearly distinguished.

the Navy, supported by Alison's battalions from Cyprus would, as the Duke informed Childers on 13 July, 'not only be most hazardous, but really quite unjustifiable by all the rules of war.' He also pointed out that, even if the Government's object was merely the protection of the Canal, Egypt would construe any landing as an act of aggression and would be likely to resist; consequently the small force envisaged by the Prime Minister must be backed up by a large one, 15,000 men from home and the Mediterranean, and another 5000 from India. Plans for the assembly and despatch of such a force had already been worked out in the War Office. Three days before the Duke's memorandum, Childers had informed the Queen that a force of two infantry divisions, a cavalry brigade, forty-eight guns and a siege train, with all the necessary transport including locomotives and rolling stock, could be landed in Egypt four to five weeks from the date of mobilisation. Tents, fuel, mules and a hospital were being made ready in Cyprus and another hospital in Malta. Royal Engineers were earmarked for railway duties, military police and a postal unit organised, a staff for handling newspaper correspondents nominated, and the scale of ammunition and rations fully worked out. In addition, arrangements had been made with the Indian Government for the despatch of its force to Suez. Childers pressed the military view upon his colleagues and, as has been seen, on 20 July the Cabinet agreed Wolseley's plan and the calling-out of the necessary reserves.

Wolseley perceived that the threat of Arabi's revolt to the continued safe functioning of the Canal could only be overcome by the crushing of that revolt at its centre, Cairo. From the capital was drawn off, from the Nile, the whole freshwater supply on which both Alexandria and the Canal's operating stations depended, as would depend any protective force. From Cairo, a freshwater canal ran out north-east across the desert to Aabasa, ten miles east of Zagazig, then on due east to Nefisha, where it forked, one branch to Ismailia on the Canal, whence pipes carried it north to Port Said, the other south to Suez. Whoever controlled the source of this water supply in Cairo controlled the Canal.

Above: British and Indian officers and men of the Indian Army regiments that formed the contingent for Egypt. Numbered from left the regiments are: Madras Sappers and Miners (1, 7); 2nd Bengal Cavalry (2, 17); 7th Bengal Infantry (3, 11); 6th Bengal Cavalry (4, 15); 20th Punjab Infantry (5,10); 29th Bombay Infantry (Baluchis) (6, 12, 14); 13th Bengal Lancers (8, 9, 13, 16). Watercolour by Orlando Norie.

Below: Lieutenant-General Sir Garnet Wolseley (in forage cap) and his staff in Egypt.

Admiral Sir Anthony Hoskins who commanded the Naval forces which secured the Canal from Port Said southwards prior to the landing of the Expeditionary Force. Photograph c 1895.

Vital though it was, therefore, to seize the Canal to prevent its destruction, such a step must be followed as soon as possible by an advance on Cairo.

There were only two practicable routes to Cairo which afforded both a freshwater supply and a railway line: from Alexandria or from Ismailia. From the start Wolseley decided on the latter. It was shorter, 75 miles as opposed to 120, it was convenient for the junction of the home force and the force from India, and it offered better going, across predominantly hard desert, than did the Nile delta which was cultivated and seamed with countless irrigation

47

works. The use of Ismailia as a base of operations would need a rapid and effective seizure of the Canal to permit the passage of the troop transports. Since the waterway could be blocked at a number of points, secrecy as to British intentions was crucial. This could best be achieved by inducing Arabi to believe that Alexandria was the intended base of operations. Although it had never been envisaged that troops would be landed at Alexandria, the decision taken by Alison to land with his battalions on 17 July now helped to deceive Arabi into the belief that this force was the spearhead of a larger one that would be disembarked to attack his Kafr-ed-Dauar position. Seymour and Alison were warned on 24 July to be ready to seize the Canal from Port Said to Ismailia in case Arabi tried to sabotage it, but on the 31st Alison was ordered to 'keep Arabi constantly alarmed'. This he proceeded to do by reconnaissances in force against Kafr-ed-Dauar. The Egyptian entrenchments according to an officer were, 'strong in front (affording) no cover for about 1000 yards, except on the right, but the Arabs can't see well and shoot very badly, though they fight fairly well.' Alison's efforts were considerably and unwittingly helped by the foreign correspondents in Alexandria whose newspapers daily exaggerated the scope and intentions of his operations.

The day before Alison received this signal, the first transport, *Orient*, sailed from the Albert Dock with the two headquarters of the 1st Division and the Guards Brigade and the 1st Scots Guards on board. They were followed on the next two days by the 2nd Grenadiers and 2nd Coldstream Guards from Ireland. Wolseley himself sailed on 2 August in company with the composite Household Cavalry Regiment, formed of one squadron each of the 1st and 2nd Life Guards and the Royal Horse Guards, going on active service for the first time since Waterloo. Thereafter, until 19 August, nine days after the Scots Guards reached Alexandria, the ships pulled out from English and Irish ports, carrying the home-based element of Wolseley's Army Corps: three more cavalry regiments, seven infantry battalions, twelve artillery batteries and an ammunition column, five companies of engineers with detachments for manning pontoons, railways and the telegraph, commissariat and medical troops; 781 officers, 15,635 men and 5847 horses in 45 ships. From the Mediterranean garrisons of Gibraltar, Malta and Cyprus sailed another seven battalions, some 7600 men. On 9 August more transports left Bombay with three regiments of Indian cavalry, the 1st Seaforth Highlanders, 1st Manchesters and three Indian battalions, a field and a mountain battery, and two companies of Madras Sappers and Miners; in all nearly another 7000 men and 1600 horses.

Thus England's might went forth. As the transports ploughed across the Mediterranean and the Indian Ocean, and as Alison's soldiers, seamen and marines skirmished against Arabi's defences, so did ships of the Royal Navy steam into position at either end of the Canal, Admiral Hoskins at Port Said, Admiral Hewett at Suez; HMS *Orion* had been in the Canal off Ismailia since 27 July. Between 12–14 August the Guards Brigade, part of the Household Cavalry and A/1 Battery Royal Artillery disembarked at Alexandria, followed on the 15th by Wolseley himself. The campaign was about to begin.

4

Landfall and Advance

As soon as the Suez Canal had been secured by the Royal Navy, Wolseley planned to land the expeditionary force at Ismailia. From there the Sweetwater Canal and the railway running west to Cairo would be seized, to within striking distance of the position which intelligence sources had reported was being prepared for the eastern defence of the Nile delta at Tel-el-Kebir; the place at which Wolseley had predicted he would defeat Arabi. When these lines of communication and water supply had been secured, and repaired if necessary, and once a sufficient accumulation of supplies and ammunition permitted, the expeditionary force would be launched at the Tel-el-Kebir position. This, it was hoped, would break the enemy's will to continue resistance, thus allowing a rapid advance and capture of Cairo, and the seizure of other places at which the remaining, outlying detachments of the Egyptian Army might concentrate.

So vulnerable were both the Maritime and Sweetwater Canals to sabotage, and so insecure was Alexandria where everything had to take place in full view of the inhabitants and an extensive press corps, that the need for a simultaneous capture of all vital points along the Maritime Canal, plus a deception plan to conceal the force's true objective, were essential if the move to Ismailia was to take Arabi by surprise. Furthermore the Canal was only wide enough for single-ship, one-way traffic, except at the *gares* (or stations) cut into the banks at intervals, thus posing navigational problems for the ships' captains, many of whom had not travelled it before and whose ships lacked the special steering gear the Canal required; in addition, the normal canal pilots were all under the control of Ferdinand de Lesseps, who was bitterly hostile to the expedition. Once the transports reached Lake Timsah, they would

have to anchor off Ismailia, which had only one small pier for disembarkation to which all the men, horses, guns and stores would have to be ferried by barges and lighters. Once ashore there was the Sweetwater Canal to be crossed, over which there was only one narrow bridge.

To overcome the navigational problems a

Vice-Admiral Sir John Fisher, who as Captain RN controlled the passage of the Expeditionary Force down the Canal to Ismailia. Later the famous First Sea Lord at the outbreak of war in 1914.

An important element of the Expeditionary Force, NCOs of No. 26 Company, Royal Engineers. The sergeant, second left, is dressed for mounted duties.

Royal Navy officer was to accompany each transport, and control of the passage was confined to one officer, Captain Fisher RN, using Thornycroft torpedo-boats which could travel up and down in the shallow water near the banks. Stores for improving the landing facilities had been prepared in England by the Royal Engineers, but of course these could not be got ashore until enough fighting troops to seize the railway and Sweetwater canal had been landed, together with the supplies necessary for their maintenance. The order of march of the transports, the timing of their passage and disembarkation would therefore require very careful planning and nice judgement. Even so, the build-up at Ismailia would inevitably take time until the facilities there could be improved.

To distract the Egyptians from these arrangements, which were worked out by Wolseley and Admiral Seymour on 16 August, everything was done to give the impression that the objective of the expeditionary force was the Kafr-ed-Dauar position against which Alison, now reinforced by the 2nd Duke of Cornwall's Light Infantry and a wing of the 1st Royal Sussex, had continued to demonstrate. The Guards Brigade under the Queen's son, the Duke of Connaught, was entrenched about Ramleh, a straggling collection of looted and deserted suburban villas between Alexandria and Aboukir Bay. The Guards had reservations about the Duke, formerly of the 60th Rifles, suspecting him, as Lieutenant Balfour of the Scots Guards noted, of 'a Rifleman's jealousy of them', but at least during the voyage out Balfour had found him 'very inoffensive and doesn't get in the way like Tum-Tum (the Prince of Wales) at a ball but chats and laughs familiarly with us all.'

Alison and his troops now came under Lieutenant-General Hamley, a quick-tempered man noted for his military writings and designated to command the 2nd Division. Hamley

The Sergeant-Major (centre back) and NCOs of 2nd Battalion, Duke of Cornwall's Light Infantry, which was landed to reinforce the Alexandria garrison demonstrating against Arabi's positions at Kafr-ed-Dauar.

was ordered to work out plans with Alison and his other brigadier, Evelyn Wood, for a frontal attack on Kafr-ed-Dauar to be made in conjunction with a flank attack by the rest of the Army after its landing in Aboukir Bay, the scene of Nelson's victory and Abercrombie's landing eighty-one years before. Everyone, including the Press, was led to believe this was the choice of landfall. Only Wolseley's chief-of-staff and second-in-command, Sir John Adye, knew the true objective.

On 18 August the Guards Brigade and such cavalry and artillery as had been landed were re-embarked, and the following afternoon the mixed fleet of ironclads and transports sailed out of Alexandria harbour. Aboard were Wolseley and Seymour, the Headquarters staff, most of the 1st Division, part of the Cavalry Brigade, over a thousand marines, two batteries, engineers and ancillary troops. At 4 pm. the ships anchored in Aboukir Bay where they remained until nightfall. Then, covered by the gunboats opening fire on the shore defences, they slipped quietly away towards Port Said,

arriving off the entrance to the Canal just after sunrise.

Meanwhile the Navy's simultaneous seizure of the Canal's vital points and its clearance of shipping was already under way. As a first step, Admiral Hewett at Suez had stopped any ship entering the southern end of the Canal on the 19th. After dark on the same day Commander Edwards of HMS *Ready* began taking over all barges and dredgers between Port Said and Ismailia and made all ships in the waterway move into the *gares*. He also occupied the Kantara telegraph station which linked Port Said with Ismailia. The attacks on the two latter places went in at about 3 am on the 20th under Captains Fairfax of HMS *Monarch* and Fitzroy of HMS *Orion* respectively. At Port Said the Egyptian sentries were quickly overpowered by a small detachment of marines, after which

Major-General HRH the Duke of Connaught and Strathearn, commanding the 1st (Guards) Brigade of the 1st Division. He was the third son of Queen Victoria.

seamen from *Monarch* and *Iris* established a cordon across the neck of land on which the town was situated to prevent any escape. Two companies of Royal Marines then surrounded the barracks and captured the Egyptian troops in their beds. At Ismailia about 500 marines and seamen from *Orion*, *Northumberland* and *Coquette* overcame the guards on the lock and at the Governor's house, and dispersed some troops outside the town all within an hour. Messages found in the telegraph office indicated that the Egyptians were intending to re-

inforce their 2000-strong garrison at Nefisha, whereupon Fitzroy ordered *Orion* and *Carysfort* to open fire on the station there; this succeeded in wrecking a train and causing such havoc in the nearby camp that the Egyptians abandoned it. To deter any counter-attack, a telegram was sent in the traffic manager's name to the Cairo War Ministry to the effect that, as 5000 British troops had landed at Ismailia, it was too late to attempt any relief; this news was acknowledged by Cairo and passed on to all concerned!

The task of the Suez force, which included the 1st Seaforth Highlanders, was the capture of the locks at Shaluf and Serapeum, either end of the Bitter Lakes. Shaluf was particularly important, as a lock on the adjoining freshwater canal had been opened by the Egyptians and if this was not closed Suez would be deprived of its water supply. This was quickly accomplished by a company of the Seaforth which then came under fire from the west bank of the freshwater canal. Lieutenant Lang swam across, secured a boat and got his men over to the far bank. Covered by fire from HMS *Seagull* and *Mosquito*, the Highlanders dispersed the enemy taking sixty-two prisoners and a quantity of ammunition. Serapeum was not occupied until the next day, but by the time Wolseley arrived off Port Said the Canal was safely in British hands.

All was now ready for the passage of the transports to Ismailia, and the advance northwards of the Indian contingent once that was concentrated at Suez. Because of the dangers of grounding – and thus blocking the Canal for the following ships – each vessel would have to proceed with caution so that a quick dash down the waterway was out of the question. However Fitzroy's small naval force at Ismailia required urgent reinforcement in case of attack from the west along the railway, so a wing of the 1st Royal West Kent was hurriedly despatched by torpedo-boat and gunboat together with Major-General Graham who was to take command at Ismailia. This done, the convoy began its journey.

Back at Alexandria the day had begun with an unpleasant shock for General Hamley, who was about to launch his 2nd Division at Kafr-ed-

Men of 1st Battalion, Queen's Own Royal West Kent Regiment, the first infantry landed to reinforce Fitzroy's seamen and marines holding Ismailia.

Dauar but first had to open a sealed letter from Wolseley, handed to him the day before with orders not to read it until early on the 20th. As he took in the opening words – 'I do not mean to land at Aboukir; my real destination is Ismailia' – Hamley was enraged at being hoodwinked, seeing his commander's deception as a lack of trust; fortunately he was unaware of the amusement Wolseley had derived from the thought of him earnestly planning an attack that would never take place. Even so there would be bad feeling between Hamley and Wolseley from that moment on, despite the latter's promise to 'bring you on as soon as I can, as I shall want every available man I can get for my fight near Tel-el-Kebir if Arabi will only in kindness stay to fight me there.' In the meantime Hamley was to tell no-one of Wolseley's true intent but to continue to distract the defenders of Kafr-ed-Dauar.

Since Wolseley estimated that Arabi had up to 9000 regular troops in position there, about a third of the total effective Egyptian strength in Wolseley's personal view, it was important to prevent them from being deployed elsewhere before sufficient force was built up at Ismailia. Wolseley's own estimate of Egyptian numbers was considerably less than that deduced by his Intelligence Department who believed that by calling up all reserves, some of them over fifty years old, the peacetime establishment of 9000 had been increased to 60,000 and some 6000 tribesmen; more than half the regulars being deployed along the north coast between Kafr-ed-Dauar and Damietta, 11,000 at Cairo, and 12,000 on the eastern side of the Delta around Tel-el-Kebir. Wolseley made light of these figures, calling his intelligence gatherers 'such wild people', and was confident that 'whether he (Arabi) has a mob of thirty thousand or a hundred thousand ... with our two divisions and the Indian contingent, the whole of Egypt assembled at Tel-el-Kebir would be made short work of'. Once he was ashore in strength, any reduction of the Kafr-ed-Dauar defences was to be welcomed as it would enable him to bring Hamley round, leaving Alexandria to be held by a reduced garrison.

At Ismailia Graham, with the West Kents and a Marine battalion, had advanced and occupied

53

Nefisha. By the evening of 23 August most of the 1st Division infantry were ashore but, so constricting did the landing facilites prove, that of the mounted troops only the Household Cavalry and two guns of N/A Battery, Royal Horse Artillery had been landed; the 7th Dragoon Guards had begun their disembarkation but the 4th had to wait off-shore. Large

Major-General Gerald Graham, commanding the 2nd Brigade, 1st Division. A holder of the Victoria Cross, won in the Crimean War, he later commanded the Suakin Field Force in 1884 and 1885.

quantities of stores were piling up near the jetty but their distribution was delayed by the bottleneck caused by the single bridge. Furthermore, urgent work was needed on the damaged Ismailia-Suez railway on which the Indian Contingent, then disembarking, would rely; but this could neither proceed, nor the rail facilities at Ismailia be improved, until the necessary stores could be landed. The whole undertaking presented a testing exercise in the allocation of landing priorities for the disembarkation staff, but gradually the men, equipment and supplies were brought ashore and the Army began to take shape for its advance, mercifully unimpeded by the Egyptians. Their commander at Tel-el-Kebir had been taken unawares by the descent on Ismailia and had withdrawn his advanced troops to Tel-el-Maskhuta, some eleven miles from the British base.

As the disembarkation progressed, the level of the Sweetwater Canal was seen to be falling, due to the enemy having constructed a dam at Magfar, seven miles away, where the low-lying countryside made it easier for them to break down the canal banks there than further west where the banks were much higher. Wolseley's aim at this stage was to secure the railway and the canal, which afforded both fresh water and an alternative line of communication, as far as Kassassin, where he intended to concentrate for the final phase. If Ismailia was deprived of its water supply by this dam at Magfar, the campaign would be halted before it was begun. He decided to push forward immediately with such troops as were available.

At 4 am on 24 August Wolseley rode out accompanied by General Drury Lowe with the Household Cavalry, a detachment each of the 19th Hussars and the Mounted Infantry, and the two guns of N/A Battery. To give support General Graham was ordered to follow on with the 2nd York and Lancaster and some Royal Marine Artillery acting as infantry. Approaching Magfar the cavalry drove in some enemy outposts, taking a few prisoners from whom it was learned that there was another dam at Tel-el-Maskhuta, where the Egyptian infantry were holding entrenchments in force.

Escorted by the cavalry, Wolseley rode forward to reconnoitre this position. From what he saw he concluded that the enemy were likely to make a stand; but by fixing them in position with the force he had in hand, he could gain time to bring up sufficient reinforcements to push on quickly to Kassassin. Orders were sent back for Graham to hurry on and for the bringing forward of 2nd DCLI from Nefisha, and the Guards Brigade and any cavalry and artillery as were available from Ismailia.

When Graham came up, the York and Lancaster was deployed astride the railway with its left on the canal and the Marines on the right with the two RHA guns in between, the line being extended out into the desert by the cavalry with the Mounted Infantry on the extreme right. Soon after 9 am the Egyptians began a hesitant advance, first against the left where they were checked by the York and Lancaster's musketry, then against the right where the excellent marksmanship of the Mounted Infantry under Captain Hutton halted them. These probing attacks continued throughout the day but at no time did the Egyptian infantry show any

inclination to close, preferring to rely upon their artillery. Their guns, though well and accurately served, were less effective than they could have been as their shells, fitted with percussion fuses, only exploded after burying themselves deep in the sand. Wolseley held back the Horse Artillery's fire, hoping to induce the Egyptians to come on, but as the enemy fire increased, Lieutenant Hickman was ordered to engage their batteries. This he did with some success, despite having only two guns against the Egyptians' twelve and despite the intense heat and heavy sand in which his men had to work.

At 2 pm the 2nd DCLI arrived but as the afternoon wore on Wolseley realised no attack would be possible that day. The Guards, leaving Ismailia at 12.45, had only some nine miles to cover but it took them until 6.45, after the sun had set. It had been a most trying and

NCOs and men of 7th (The Princess Royal's) Dragoon Guards in their campaigning kit of scarlet serge frocks, blue pantaloons with yellow stripe, and blue puttees. The privates are armed with swords and carbines, the sergeant (standing centre) and trumpeter with swords and revolvers.

exhausting march, as Private Macauley of the Scots Guards recalled, across 'a long stretch of shifting sand on which our feet slipped backwards at every step. The hot wind that was blowing made us terribly thirsty, and soon the pint and a half which each of our water bottles held was exhausted.' Although equipped with tropical helmets, the Guards, like the other troops from England and the Mediterranean, marched in their home service scarlet and blue serge which, with 100 rounds of ammunition, haversacks and water bottles, was not best suited to temperatures in the nineties. Indeed heat and thirst had proved worse enemies than the Egyptians for all those engaged that day. Wolseley, already at odds with Hamley, had formed a dubious opinion of his other divisional commander, General Willis, 'a nice old man' in Lieutenant Balfour's view, but who had collapsed from his exertions in front of Tel-el-Maskhuta.

With the Guards had arrived the other four guns of N/A Battery, and a little earlier Drury Lowe had been reinforced by 350 sabres of the 4th and 7th Dragoon Guards. A/1 Battery, Royal Artillery and two more battalions, 3rd KRRC and Royal Marine Light Infantry, were moving up, so Wolseley gave orders for an attack next day.

The advance began at daybreak but it was soon clear that the enemy had abandoned his positions during the night so the cavalry and N/A Battery pushed on to try and cut off his retreat. Although the Mounted Infantry, on small locally-bred horses, could make good speed across the desert it was hard going for the big Heavy Cavalry troopers, who rode poor-conditioned mounts so recently landed from transports. On arriving at Mahsama station, seven miles up the line, only the enemy rearguard was found still in position. Supported by the guns, the Mounted Infantry dismounted and opened fire, followed by the cavalry charging through the station and camp. Though they were too late to cut off the enemy, the latter left behind seven Krupp guns, large numbers of rifles, a quantity of supplies and an ammunition train of seventy-five wagons. Because of the uncertainty of being able to supply troops as far

Major-General Sir D.C. Drury Lowe, commanding the Cavalry Division.

forward as Mahsama before the Sweetwater Canal dams had been cleared and the railway restored to working order, Wolseley had intended to remain at Tel-el-Maskhuta, but when informed of the captured supplies and the enemy's withdrawal he told Willis to send forward Graham's brigade through Mahsama to occupy Kassassin Lock. At daybreak on the 26th a 4th Dragoon Guards patrol found the lock deserted and later in the day Graham marched in with the 2nd DCLI, 2nd York and Lancaster and the Marine Artillery.

Wolseley had thus attained his first tactical objective earlier than he had anticipated but his

operational moves had outstripped his logistic backing. His supply situation had been eased by the captured enemy stores and the organisation by the Navy of a boat supply service along the Sweetwater canal as far as Magfar, but until the two dams and a blocking mound across the railway could be removed, and his locomotives got working on the line, a sufficiency of stores could neither be amassed at Kassassin, nor could more troops be moved forward. The numbers deployed along the line Ismailia-Kassassin, both to hold the ground gained and provide the large working parties for clearing the canal and railway, were entirely governed by the quantity of supplies that could be moved forward and distributed, which in turn depended on the transport available. Makeshift arrangements

NCOs and men of the 19th Hussars, a regiment which served in both the Egyptian expedition and the Sudan campaigns of 1884–85. The uniform is blue serge frocks, blue pantaloons with yellow stripe, and knee boots. Above their chevrons, the NCOs wear the regimental arm badge of the elephant.

had to be improvised on canal and railway but even so some of the forward troops suffered shortages due to an insufficiency of mules to draw the wheeled transport through the deep sand.

The establishment of properly functioning lines of communication and forward depots would take time and much hard work, but would allow Wolseley to assemble the rest of his force at Ismailia. Some transports of the original convoy had still to be cleared, particularly of artillery. The Indian Contingent was due to

Above: Some members of the Mounted Infantry. The men with white accoutrements are from the 1st South Staffords, the remainder from the 3rd King's Royal Rifles. Bedford cord breeches and canvas gaiters have replaced the normal blue or green trousers.

Below: Mule-drawn regimental water carts photographed after the campaign. Essential equipment for supplying the forward troops but difficult to pull through thick sand.

complete its concentration at Ismailia by the 28th, moving partly by road, partly by the Maritime Canal. Its cavalry brigade now made up a division with the British cavalry under the overall command of Drury Lowe. On the 26th Wolseley received an impatient signal from Hamley, 'Can you not tell me what you wish me to do?' In reply Hamley was ordered to leave Evelyn Wood's brigade of three and a half battalions, plus the 2nd Derbyshire and 2nd Manchester, two garrison artillery batteries and the Malta Fencibles to protect Alexandria, providing Sir Edward Malet agreed this was sufficient force; then to embark for Ismailia with the Highland Brigade (1st Black Watch, 2nd Highland Light Infantry, 1st Gordon and 1st Cameron Highlanders), now commanded ·by Alison. Having said he would be ready to leave on the 28th, Hamley then requested permission to use the Highland Brigade for an attack on the Egyptian lines; this drew a brusque, 'No; embark as soon as all ready; desire Sir E. Wood to remain on the defensive and risk nothing.' This exchange did little to improve relations between Wolseley and Hamley.

A fractious divisional commander was something Wolseley could do without on the 28th. He was concerned about the supply and transport situation, particularly the non-arrival of the locomotives, which had had to be taken all the way down to Suez since they could not be unloaded at the Ismailia jetty. The same day saw an Egyptian foray against Graham's outpost at Kassassin, which for a time had seemed to be in acute danger, according to reports reaching Headquarters.

At Kassassin Graham had a mixed detachment of 4th and 7th Dragoon Guards, his two battalions and the Marine Artillery, the Mounted Infantry and two guns of N/A, RHA, whose ammunition was limited to that in their limbers, thirty-six rounds per gun. On the morning of the 28th the enemy were spotted on some higher ground to the north and Graham alerted Drury Lowe at Mahsama. The cavalry turned out, ready to advance if need be but as the Egyptians withdrew after loosing off some ineffectual gunfire, both Graham and Lowe returned to their camps during the afternoon,

their men having been much exposed to a broiling sun. At 4.30 pm the enemy showed signs of coming on again, this time in greater strength with cavalry and infantry supported by guns, their line of attack appearing to be mainly against Graham's open right flank. Again messages went back, to Lowe asking him to cover the right, and to inform Willis at Tel-el-Maskhuta. More guns had gone forward to

Lieutenant-Colonel H.P. Ewart, 2nd Life Guards, commanding the composite Household Cavalry Regiment, who led the charge at Kassassin.

Graham in the afternoon, and now the Marine Light Infantry and another battery set off from Mahsama, while Lowe moved out with the Household Cavalry, 7th Dragoon Guards and N/A's four remaining guns. At 5.20 pm it appeared to Graham that the enemy's advance against his right would expose them to an attack in flank by Lowe. Accordingly he sent off his ADC, Lieutenant Pirie, with a verbal message asking Lowe to take the cavalry round by Graham's right and attack the left flank of the Egyptian skirmishers. Graham's infantry and guns were steadily engaging the enemy where they showed but the light was failing and the ammunition with the guns was running low, owing to the difficulties of bringing forward the reserve ammunition waggons in the thick sand. Graham, however, was unperturbed, thinking it unlikely that the Egyptians would press their attack, particularly after dark, and by 7.15, when the Marines marched in with A/1 Battery, he ordered an advance to coincide, he hoped, with Lowe's flank attack.

Meanwhile Pirie, having failed to find Lowe at the place to which he had been directed and conscious of the urgency of his task, had been growing increasingly worried as he galloped through the falling darkness in search of the cavalry. To make matters worse his horse foundered from exhaustion and his anxiety mounted as the precious time slipped past. Fortunately he ran into a battery returning from Kassassin out of ammunition. He borrowed a horse and rode off again, but even more perturbed by the implications of that now-ineffective battery. Knowing what his general intended Pirie had some idea where to look for the elusive cavalry and eventually caught up with them some four miles north-west of Kassassin. By now in a highly excitable state, he hurriedly blurted out his orders for Lowe to attack the enemy left as quickly as possible because Graham 'was only just able to hold his own'.

To Lowe, therefore, it seemed as though he might be riding into a night action which could by now be lost. Nevertheless he wheeled his brigade round and advanced in a wide sweep to come in on the enemy's left, the 7th Dragoon

Guards leading, the guns behind and the Household Cavalry in the second line. A thick haze covered the desert but a bright moon was shining and the flash and sound of the firing around Kassassin afforded some aid to direction. Suddenly they came under artillery and rifle fire from straight ahead. Lowe immediately ordered the Dragoons to clear the front of the four 13-pounders. They wheeled off right and left to form again behind the second line, as the horse gunners rapidly unlimbered and opened fire. The Household Cavalry, all three squadrons in line, rode up on the right of the guns and, on Lowe's order, charged straight at the front of the Egyptian infantry. To the luckless fellah conscripts, tired after the day's action, their white uniforms all too conspicuous in the moonlight, the awe-inspiring sight of that thundering phalanx of huge, cheering men in scarlet and blue, their faces dark and menacing under the helmets, must have caused even the bravest spirits to look over their shoulders. But there was no time, no place to run. In seconds the massive black horses were plunging into and over their quavering line, the long, heavy swords rising and falling as they cut and stabbed, until what shortly before had been a formed body deployed for action was well-nigh obliterated by the speed and weight of the charge. Seeing their infantry annihilated, the Egyptian gunners beyond and their cavalry further away to their left made off into the desert before the victorious Life Guardsmen and Blues could reform to charge again. The 7th Dragoon Guards, who had caught the first enemy fire, lost two killed, including an officer, and three wounded, while the Household Cavalry had seven killed and fourteen wounded; twenty horses were killed and another twenty-three injured. At 8.15 a Life Guards officer reported the successful charge to Kassassin and half an hour later Graham withdrew his troops to camp.

Over the next twelve days, as the railway was put into working order and the enemy positions at Tel-el-Kebir were reconnoitred, more troops and supplies were moved forward so that the whole corps, including the Highland Brigade and the Indian Contingent, would be

Above: The moonlight charge of the Household Cavalry and 7th Dragoon Guards at Kassassin, 28 August 1882. *Left*: The moment of impact. *Right*: Life Guards rallying after the charge. Engravings for the *Illustrated London News* after R. Caton Woodville, who was a war artist with the Expedition.

Below: Officers of the 13th Bengal Lancers, whose patrols first reported the Egyptian advance on 9 September.

7/1 Mountain Battery, Royal Artillery, part of the Indian Contingent, in action at Kassassin on 9 September. The gunners are British, the muleteers Indian. An engraving for the *Illustrated London News*.

concentrated at Kassassin by 12 September. Wolseley's own headquarters was due to move there from Ismailia on the 9th.

As Wolseley was preparing to set out, a message came through that Kassassin was under attack. By this time Arabi himself was present at Tel-el-Kebir and, on learning from his Arab scouts that the British position was weakly held and that they had cut the communications to Ismailia, he decided upon a combined attack from Tel-el-Kebir and Es Salihiyeh, fifteen miles north of Kassassin. As it happened Arabi had been completely misled, for Willis, now commanding at Kassassin, had a well-balanced force of all arms 8000 strong, with the Guards Brigade and 4th Dragoon Guards only ten miles away at Tel-el-Maskhuta. As soon as the early morning patrols of the 13th Bengal Lancers reported the enemy's advance, Graham's brigade, now mustering six battalions and three batteries, took up positions on both banks of the Sweetwater Canal facing west, with the right wing com-posed of the 2nd Royal Irish and 2nd DCLI thrown back to confront the enemy thrust from Es Salihiyeh. The two cavalry brigades advanced to delay and keep separate the two enemy forces. At the same time Willis ordered the Guards to advance and strike the northern attack on its left flank.

About an hour after these deployments had been made, and with the Egyptians once more showing reluctance to press home their attacks, Willis ordered a general advance. Shelled by the artillery, the Egyptians did not wait for the infantry or cavalry and retreated back whence they had come. By 10.30 am Graham's battalions were within 5000 yards of the Tel-el-Kebir defences and came under fire from the Egyptian artillery. Had the advance pushed on, the enemy positions might have been carried, though not without considerable loss; but as the force was neither sufficiently concentrated nor supplied for any pursuit, the troops were withdrawn to Kassassin. At 4 pm the Guards Brigade sullenly marched in. Three times now they had been called upon to advance at best speed in the heat of the day, only to find on arrival they were not required. Apart from that, they had done nothing in the campaign so far except, as Balfour of the Scots Guards wrote bitterly, 'dig out blocks on railways and canals and load and unload trains while regiment after regiment goes on to the front'. It seems to have crossed some guardsmen's minds that their distance from the front may have been occasioned by fears for the safety of their Royal commander. In fact Wolseley was concerned more about the Duke of Connaught's stamina than his safety, but since the Duke's appointment had been instigated by Wolseley in an attempt to improve his own standing in Court circles, he really had only himself to blame for the Duke's presence with the army.

5

Wolseley Attacks

With the arrival of 1st Royal Irish Fusiliers on the afternoon of 12 September the army corps was now fully concentrated for the final blow at Arabi's forces in the field. Careful reconnaissances had revealed that the enemy positions began at a point on the Sweetwater Canal a mile and a quarter in front of Tel-el-Kebir station and bridge, and some six miles from Kassassin. They consisted of a continuous line of earthworks running north into the desert for about four miles with ten redoubts of varying size at intervals. The strongest sections were in the vicinity of the canal and railway, where there were ten guns; the centre with two redoubts 1100 yards apart, one with four guns, the other with five; and the northern extremity where a total of seven guns were in two more redoubts similarly spaced. Some 1000 yards in front of the entrenchments and 1600 yards north of the canal was an advanced redoubt with eight guns and infantry. From the east this was concealed by rising ground, and although its existence had been perceived by British observers from the south-east, the mirage effect and the angle from which it was seen made it appear as part of the main position. Its true location was therefore unknown to Wolseley. Behind the main position the Egyptians had constructed further entrenchments mounting twenty-four guns, which ran back for 3500 yards from roughly the centre of their main line and faced north-west to protect their camps. These were not visible from the east, and their centre was some three miles from the nearest point on the north flank reached by British patrols, so little, if any knowledge of them was available.

From previous experience it was known that the Egyptians were capable of strong and well-constructed earthworks. The whole line was fronted by a ditch with sloping sides whose dimensions averaged six feet deep by nine feet wide at the surface, though in front of the gun redoubts the ditch was much wider and deeper, with outside it another rampart and a shallower ditch. The built-up ramparts and batteries behind the ditch were generally between five to six feet high, and four to ten feet thick at the top, widening towards the base with sloping fronts. They were built of sand, revetted with weeds and mud. These formed substantial obstacles for assaulting infantry to negotiate under fire at close range. So far in the campaign the Egyptian infantry's offensive qualities had not been impressive and, though well-armed with modern Remington rifles – single-shot breechloaders like the British Martini-Henry – the accuracy of their musketry was erratic. However, fighting from strong positions in close proximity to the 9- and 14-pounder Krupp guns of their artillery – an arm considered by Wolseley to be the 'only good branch of the Egyptian army' – the infantry conscripts might well prove more resolute in defence. For all that, it had been observed that the Egyptians only threw out a protective screen forward of the position at daybreak. Wolseley's estimate of the enemy strength was some 30,000 and 60–70 guns, which was slightly in excess of the figures given by Arabi after the war of 20,000 regulars, 2000 tribesmen and seventy-five guns. Fourteen battalions were posted in or close to the main position, three were in reserve and three more were deployed slightly forward south of the canal.

The approach to Arabi's lines south of the canal was across cultivated land scattered with small villages until the town of Tel-el-Kebir itself was reached. The terrain alongside the railway and canal was loose sand but north of the railway the ground rose for about a mile to a height of 130 feet, levelling out on to a plateau

Bird's eye view of the attack on Arabi's position at Tel-el-Kebir, 13 September 1882. The main Egyptian line is shrouded with smoke. Behind it is the enemy camp protected by its entrenchments running back to the Tel-el-Kebir bridge over the Sweetwater Canal. The town itself is visible in the distance on the far side of the Canal. The British troops are attacking in the left foreground.

of hard sandy gravel which ran from Kassassin, rising very slightly as it approached the Egyptian lines. Though it afforded good going for infantry and guns, it was completely devoid of cover and gave the defenders excellent fields of fire.

In view of all these factors, and the need to give the cavalry as much daylight as possible for the pursuit to Cairo, Wolseley decided upon a night advance due west across the plateau, followed by a break-in to the defences at first light by his two infantry divisions. The whole attack was to be silent, with no preliminary bombardment, but with artillery advancing between the divisions ready to support the attack as soon as surprise was lost. Each division would move with one brigade forward, the other in reserve 1000 yards behind; the frontage of each assaulting brigade was to be 1000 yards, with an interval of 1200 yards between the inner flanks of each division. On the left, Hamley's 2nd Division, with the Highland Brigade leading, was to move with its left 2000 yards from and parallel to the railway; since this division's other brigade had been left at Alexandria its reserve was formed of the 2nd DCLI and 3rd KRRC under the command of the latter's Colonel Ashburnham. The rising ground between the railway and the division's left was to be watched by two squadrons of the 19th Hussars. On the right, Graham's brigade (RMLI, 1st Royal Irish Fusiliers, 2nd York and Lancaster, and 2nd Royal Irish Regiment) would lead the 1st Division's attack with the Guards Brigade in reserve. The seven field batteries (forty-two guns) were to advance in line, keeping station with the reserve brigades. The Cavalry Division, with two RHA batteries, was to move to the right rear of the 1st Division, ready to swing round the Egyptian open, north flank once the infantry had broken in.

A representative group of 1st Battalion, Black Watch (Royal Highlanders) in the dress and equipment as worn at Tel-el-Kebir. From left: Piper McDonald, Sergeant-Major Young, Privates Scobbie, Stewart, Smith, Sharp, Colour-Sergeant Watt, Drummer Slattie.

Wolseley's headquarters, escorted by the Royal Marine Artillery, would follow the 2nd Division.

South of the canal the Indian Infantry Brigade (1st Seaforth Highlanders, 7th Bengal Infantry, 20th Punjabis, 29th Baluchis), with one squadron 6th Bengal Cavalry and a mountain battery, was to begin its advance an hour after the main advance had started, so as to avoid alerting the villagers in the cultivated area, and was to be ready to press ahead and seize the important railway junction of Zagazig, fifteen miles west of Tel-el-Kebir. It was to have the additional support of a Naval Brigade under Captain Fitzroy RN with six Gatling guns and a 40-pounder mounted on the railway. This was to be followed by 17th Company, Royal Engineers, a pontoon troop on the canal, a field ambulance and hospital.

When darkness had fallen the camp tents were struck and the troops moved out to take up their assault formations on the start line marked by posts lined up by the Royal Engineers. It was extremely dark and it was not until 11 pm that all was ready. As the troops rested Wolseley rode round the assembled force. Smoking, lights, loud orders were forbidden, rifles were to be unloaded, and no bugles or pipes were to sound until after daybreak. Navigation was to be by the stars and a Naval officer skilled in this task, Lieutenant Rawson, was to give the direction from the centre of the Highland Brigade, which was arrayed with all four battalions in line, each battalion having four companies forward and four in support.

At 1.30 am the whole mass moved silently forward at a steady pace. Keeping direction and alignment proved difficult, there being no moon, much cloud and only the North Star and Great Bear constantly visible. After an hour and a half's marching a halt was ordered to rest the men. In the Highland Brigade the command, passed quietly down the line, took time to reach

Above: The Sergeant-Major, NCOs and a piper of 1st Battalion, Gordon Highlanders, which formed the right centre of the Highland Brigade at Tel-el-Kebir. This was one of the battalions equipped with black leather ammunition pouches instead of the more usual buff.

Below: The Black Watch advancing under fire at Tel-el-Kebir. An engraving after R. Caton Woodville. Although the dress depicted is broadly correct, errors have occurred in the engraving, for example, the white stripe in the kilts, and the mess-tin carried between the shoulder blades being drawn more like a pouch.

the flanks which marched on so that the brigade halted in a crescent. When the advance was resumed the outer companies edged inwards, nearly meeting in the centre, and another halt had to be made for the formation to be re-aligned. At about the same time Graham's brigade altered its formation so that all its companies were in line in case the enemy was suddenly bumped, but so unwieldy did this prove in the darkness that each company was ordered to advance in fours. Since this was undoubtedly the first night attack the troops had ever participated in, it was surprising that more noise and confusion did not result. As it was, an officer noted that 'sound or sight at 100 yards from any column there was none.'

As time wore on the stars veered north-west and consequently the lines of advance unwittingly followed suit, drawing both divisions off their intended axes. This had two unforeseen advantages. Graham's men were now heading towards a weaker section of the Egyptian line than they would otherwise have encountered, while the Highlanders' march took them out of the path of the advanced redoubt, of whose

Types of 2nd Battalion, Highland Light Infantry, the battalion which encountered some of the stiffest Egyptian resistance on the left of the Highland Brigade's attack. In 1882 this battalion was still wearing trews of the old 74th tartan. Only its pipers were kilted.

position they were unaware and whose garrison would have alerted the whole enemy line earlier.

In the event surprise was not lost. At about 4.55 an Egyptian picquet some 200 yards in front of the entrenchment spotted the silent lines of Highlanders looming out of the darkness and fired warning shots. The Highlanders fixed bayonets without halting and quietly increased their pace as the alarmed Egyptians awoke and rushed to their parapets. At about 150 yards range the whole entrenchment blazed fire from end to end. With bugles blaring the advance, the Black Watch, Gordons, Camerons and Highland Light Infantry charged cheering and yelling, as their pipers hurriedly inflated the bags of their pipes to spur on their comrades. On the right the 1st Division had still been some 700 yards short of its objective when the alarm was given, so had to advance under fire longer than the Highlanders, at the same time deploying from fours into assault formation. For the first ten minutes or so, therefore, Alison's men had to fight alone in the entrenchments.

At first the Egyptians resisted fiercely, pouring a heavy fire into the Highlanders clambering out of the ditch and up the slithering scarps of the ramparts. In the centre, led from the front by Alison, the Gordons and Camerons forced an entry with bullet and bayonet, but so heavy was the fire at close range that some of their men began to fall back and had to be rallied by Hamley himself who quickly came forward with the reserve companies. His leadership and these reinforcements so stiffened the embattled assault companies that the front trench was successfully cleared. Thereupon Hamley led the two battalions on into the double line of rearward, north-westerly facing trenches where again the fire was intense. With the open ground swept by musketry and artillery, the Highlanders had to fight their way down the trenches from end to end. While the Gordons and Camerons pushed on, the flank battalions were meeting tougher resistance. On the right the Black Watch was confronted by the big 5-gun redoubt defended by a double line of emplacements strongly held, which took some 25 minutes of close-quarter fighting and some help from the Rifles in reserve to finally overcome. On the left the Highland Light Infantry came up against a 4-gun redoubt protected by a very wide and deep ditch which proved difficult to cross, defended as it was by Sudanese troops who fought with ferocity, counter-attacking resolutely. The HLI's first attack failed and it was not until the DCLI came up in support that the position was finally carried after about three-quarters of an hour of the fiercest fighting of the whole attack. Here it was that the only Victoria Cross subsequently awarded for the battle was won by Lieutenant Edwards of the HLI, who charged alone into a battery to encourage his men.

Meanwhile, on the 1st Division front, Graham's scarlet lines, edged on the left by the Marines' blue[1], stormed their trenches with a rush and were quickly into them. However, as the charging troops came over the parapets, the enemy fell back a short distance and poured fire into the packed, excited ranks of the attackers, who suffered casualties, particularly amongst the Marines. The enemy infantry was also being supported by the guns in the redoubt attacked by the Black Watch, but as soon as these were silenced, N/2 Battery Royal Artillery managed to drive its 16-pounders over the entrenchments close by and, though one gun broke a wheel, two guns went into action to support Graham's renewed attack.[2] The Royal Irish on the right advanced in short rushes to close with the enemy who, now under N/2's fire and seeing Graham's other battalions coming on again, with the hitherto uncommitted Guards Brigade behind, began to break away towards the rear. N/2's other three guns were at this time firing in support of the Gordons and Camerons fighting down the inner trenches. Meanwhile A/1 and D/1 Batteries, without crossing the trenches, had opened enfilade fire on the unattacked defences to Graham's left, as the Black Watch and part of the Rifles wheeled right to threaten the rear of the same positions.

The enemy left now crumbled rapidly, for the Cavalry Division, with the Indian Brigade leading and the Horse Artillery engaging the extreme northern redoubt, swept round the flank and started to ride down the rear of the defences, driving the fleeing Egyptian left towards the Tel-el-Kebir bridge. By 5.30 am, with all resistance overcome, Graham's brigade and the Guards, who though exposed to fire had not been engaged, advanced in the same direction. Seeing their left collapse, the Egyptians who had been resisting the Gordons and Camerons took to their heels, followed by the remaining defenders of the 4-gun redoubt which was finally captured by the HLI and DCLI at 5.40. These two battalions turned south to clear the remaining works down to the canal. By 6 o'clock all resistance on the main line had ceased and the victorious British were converging on the bridge.

---

[1] Although the RMLI's full dress was scarlet, their undress in which they fought was blue.

[2] For this exploit N/2 and its successor batteries in the Royal Artillery have borne the subsidiary title of 'The Broken Wheel Battery'.

N/2 Battery, Royal Artillery driving its guns over the Egyptian defences, the exploit which gained it the title of the 'Broken Wheel Battery'. Watercolour by John Charlton.

Men of N/2 Battery, Royal Artillery. From left: Battery-Sergeant-Major Chapman, Bombardier Bates, Trumpeter Beatie, Gunner Smith, Driver Bishop, Bombardier Bond, Corporal Reed, Sergeant Stoyle, Gunner McIntosh, Driver Lane. The mounted NCOs, trumpeter and drivers wear pantaloons and knee boots, the gunners trousers. The Battery dog's name was Jack.

South of the canal the Indian Infantry Brigade had come under fire at about 5.10. Supported by the Naval Gatlings, the 1st Seaforth attacked in front while the 20th Punjabis swung out left and came in on the enemy's right flank. The Egyptians gave way and the squadron of the 6th Cavalry rode forward to cut off the fugitives pouring into Tel-el-Kebir town from the north.

At 7 am Wolseley rode on to the bridge amid his cheering soldiers. His victory was complete: the set-piece night attack, a novel operation for its time, had been entirely successful, Arabi had fled, his army was broken and demoralised with 2000 killed and unknown numbers wounded, all at the place and more or less the time Wolseley had predicted before leaving England. British casualties had been 57 killed and 412 wounded and missing, the heaviest loss being sustained by the Highland Brigade who had 45 killed (including 6 officers) and 186 wounded, its hardest-hit battalion being the 2nd HLI with 17 killed and 57 wounded; the Marines in Graham's brigade, however, suf-

Opposite: 2nd Battalion, Royal Irish Regiment fighting its way into the Egyptian defences. Painting by C.J. Marshman.

Opposite below: HRH the Duke of Connaught (on grey) with the Guards Brigade waiting in reserve to the 1st Division's attack. Painting by R. Caton Woodville.

Below: Officers and men of the 20th Punjab Infantry, the left forward battalion of the Indian Contingent's attack. Its uniform was 'drab' with green facings.

fered 80 casualties, the largest number for any battalion in the whole corps. The Guards, though coming under fire and losing one man killed, had again been deprived of their chance and Lieutenant Balfour had to console himself with the thought that 'we were in reserve at the point where it was most necessary that the attack should succeed', finding some pride in the fact that the guardsmen outmarched Graham's brigade in the race to the bridge; possibly he found it difficult to accept that it was the hard fighting of the two Irish battalions, the York and Lancasters and the Marines which had ensured the Guards were still fresh and almost unscathed.

Wolseley's conviction that one decisive action would break the Egyptians' will to continue the struggle was now proved correct. The Indian Infantry Brigade pressed on to occupy Zagazig without difficulty, even marching par-

Opposite: Sir Garnet Wolseley and staff cheered by victorious Gordon and Cameron Highlanders as he arrives at Tel-el-Kebir bridge. After the painting by Lady Butler, whose husband, then Lieutenant-Colonel W.F. Butler, was on Wolseley's staff.

Above: Indian Cavalry pursuing the defeated Egyptians after Tel-el-Kebir. Engraving after R. Caton Woodville.

Opposite below: Some of the wounded convalescing after the campaign. Apart from the two Highlanders, the others are in hospital 'blues' and woollen 'caps comforter', an article still in service today.

allel with bodies of Egyptian soldiers from Tel-el-Kebir which, though still armed, offered no resistance. The Cavalry Division swung southwest to cover the fifty miles to Cairo at best speed with the Indian Cavalry leading the way to Belbeis, which was reached at noon when a halt was called for the day. Early next morning the advance continued amid growing demonstrations of thankfulness from the inhabitants that the fighting was over, and by late afternoon the outskirts of Cairo were reached. Since nothing was known of affairs in the city and he had only a small force immediately to hand, Drury Lowe sent forward a detachment of 4th Dragoon Guards and some Indians under Colonel Herbert Stewart. The latter found the Egyptian authorities ready to surrender but apprehensive that the entry of British troops that night might provoke a riot. Stewart insisted upon the Citadel's garrison laying down its arms and the surrender of Arabi who was known to be in the city. So it was agreed, and after dark 150 men of the 4th Dragoon Guards and Mounted Infantry took over the Citadel without passing through the main streets and supervised the piling of the garrison's weapons. In this way 10,000 Egyptian troops were disarmed without trouble and next day were permitted to disperse to their homes, doubtless grateful for this early and unexpected discharge from military service. At 10.45 that night Arabi and his second-in-command yielded their swords to Drury Lowe at the Abbasiyeh Barracks.

It only remained to secure the outlying centres of communication at which any recalcitrant Egyptian troops might concentrate, to obtain the surrender of the distant garrisons and to build up the British force in Cairo. Only at the railway junction of Tanta, a centre of anti-Christian fanaticism, was there any threat of trouble from an unruly populace and a body of soldiers unaware of the surrender in Cairo. The firm handling of a potentially ugly situation by Alison, supported by only three companies of very steady Gordon Highlanders, restored order quietly and without bloodshed. By the 24th the last surrenders had been made and on the following day the Khedive Tewfik made a ceremonial, if hardly triumphant, entry into his capital while British soldiers lined the streets. Thus within two months of the British Cabinet's decision to take military action to uphold the Khedive's authority, the object had been achieved.

It was decided that, for the time being, until Egypt was thoroughly restored to tranquillity an army of occupation, fixed at 10,000 men, would have to remain, but the balance of the expeditionary force returned to England or India. With them went Wolseley to receive his rewards for what Childers called 'the most perfect military achievement England has seen for many a long year'. The Royal Navy, always beyond criticism in Victorian England, had done everything required of it and worked harmoniously with the sister Service. The Army, whose reforms Wolseley had so consistently championed, had acquitted itself well, even if the calibre of its opponents had been less than its own. Wolseley himself had organised his campaign skilfully and expeditiously, displaying an appreciation of the importance of well-found logistic arrangements if operations were to succeed, thus overcoming the rock on which so many previous British campaigns had foundered. Confident in the merit of what he had done, he expected much in the way of recognition and consequently was piqued when this proved less than he felt was his due: promotion to full general instead of field-marshal, a barony rather than a viscountcy, a grant £5000 less than the £35,000 he had anticipated; while the Royal congratulations and acknowledgement of his services seemed, in his view, to be 'as cold-blooded an effusion as you have ever read'. Popular with the general public Wolseley may have been, competent and clever he undoubtedly was, but his arrogance and self-publicity did not endear him to the upper echelons of power and society.

As for Arabi Pasha and his chief lieutenants, the British Government agreed that they should be handed over to the Khedive for judgement but insisted that, in the Foreign Secretary's words, 'the prisoner must have a fair trial, and that no improper or unjust restrictions are placed on the defence.' Furthermore, in the event of a guilty verdict, a sentence of 'unnecessary severity' could result in a British appeal to the Khedive for clemency. Sir Edward Malet believed that a possible death penalty for the prisoners, far from buttressing the Khedivial authority, would be likely 'to canonise them and that they would, if executed, be more than before objects of veneration and fanatical enthusiasm'. Since overt British interference in Egyptian affairs would also undermine the Khedive's standing, the implementation of British wishes in the matter of Arabi had to be conducted with some subtlety and discretion. Thus it was not until 3 December that Arabi and his seven chief confederates were brought before a court-martial, charged with rebellion against the Khedive. The accused pleaded guilty and were sentenced to death, the sentence then being commuted by the Khedive to 'perpetual exile'. Arabi was transported to Ceylon, whence in 1901 he was eventually permitted to return to an Egypt which had forgotten him. He was nevertheless the first exponent of Egyptian nationalism and the forerunner of those who, in the mid-twentieth century, would bring national self-respect to Egypt.

In reluctantly agreeing to British military intervention in Egypt, no idea of annexation or long-term military occupation entered Gladstone's head. Such a policy was anathema to his Liberal principles. In any case, notwithstanding the importance of Egypt as a factor in the protection of Britain's Eastern interests – which again seemed threatened by Russian advances in Central Asia – Britain had neither the military nor financial capacity to defend Egypt permanently against external aggression or internal insurrection. The best that could be done, indeed what a Liberal Government should do, was to restore Egypt to stability, solvency and security under the Khedive and his own ministers by a complete overhaul of all Egyptian institutions, guided and assisted by British advisors inspired with British standards of justice and humanity. The civil side, begun by Lord Dufferin and Sir Edward Malet, was to be the task of Sir Evelyn Baring, who had been the British Controller-General of Finance in Cairo up to 1880. On the military side a Gendarmerie was to be organised by Colonel Valentine Baker, while a new Egyptian Army was to be raised and trained by Major-General Evelyn Wood, appointed its first Sirdar, or Commander-in-Chief. Until these forces could effectively safeguard the new Egypt, a British garrison would have to remain, though for as short a time as possible.

Such were Gladstone's intentions. In the event, so foreign did the Gladstonian ideals of just and progressive administration prove to a country inured for years to tyranny and corruption, that Baring had perforce to become the de facto ruler of Egypt if such ideals were ever to be realised. As for the security of the country, this was endangered from without before Wood's work had even begun. Indeed the threat had started to emerge in the year before Tel-el-Kebir and was gathering strength when this was fought – in Egypt's southern provinces of the Sudan.

= PART II =

THE MAHDI'S REBELLION

6

The Sudan Erupts

From its source in Central Africa the White Nile flows northwards, fed from the west by the tributary of the Bahr-el-Ghazal, until after a thousand miles it is joined by the Blue Nile which springs from the Abyssinian Highlands. At this confluence stands Khartoum. Beyond it the great river flows on, through Berber to Abu Hamed, where it abruptly turns south-west for some 200 miles and then bends northwards again, passing Dongola and Wadi Halfa, where it enters Egypt, until it reaches the last of six cataracts at Assuan. Throughout this second thousand-mile stretch the river passes through a wilderness of desert reaching from the Red Sea in the east to the Sahara, a limitless barren plain of sand broken only by tumbled piles of black rock and patches of thorn scrub. In these sun-scorched wastes rainfall is a freak of nature and, apart from some scattered wells, life can only be supported along the banks of the Nile.

Two hundred years after the foundation of Islam a great wave of Arabs poured across these lands of the Sudan, the country of the Blacks, imposing their customs, language and religion upon the indigenous inhabitants. In due course the two races became mingled but with the Arab strain always the more dominant, except in the far south where the Arabs preyed but did not settle. Some of the Arabs were nomadic camel breeders who settled chiefly in the north. Others were cattle owners, the Baggara, who spread across the more fertile lands of southern Kordofan, north of the Bahr-el-Ghazal, their avaricious eyes fixed on the equatorial belt to the south, where dwelled great herds of elephants hunted for their ivory and, most lucrative of all, the placid, ignorant, defenceless inhabitants of black Africa hunted as slaves. For centuries convoys of wretched humanity were shepherded by their cruel captors up the Nile to the north or across the Red Sea to the great slave market of Jeddah.

Cut off from the outside world by deserts and equatorial forests the Sudan was a country of disunited, feuding Arab tribes, interbreeding, harrying and enslaving the weaker but more numerous blacks, a land of animal and mineral resources in parts but without cohesion of any sort; a land ripe for a determined conqueror. In 1819 Mohammed Ali of Egypt, anxious to find employment for the unruly troops with which he had subdued the Mamelukes, and with his

Panoramic map of the River Nile from the Mediterranean to Khartoum (top). The Sudan occupies the area alongside the three small pictures at top right.

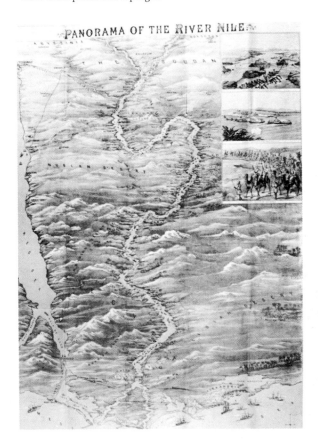

PANORAMA OF THE RIVER NILE

eye on the resources of the Sudan, sent an expedition up the Nile which overcame all resistance and established garrisons and a seat of government at Khartoum. In the following decades Egypt extended its dominion over the Sudan until by 1870 the southernmost limits of its territory had been fixed in the equatorial region, over 800 miles south of Khartoum.

In the sixty years that followed Egypt's conquest, and particularly during the last decade its rule was a saga of oppression, extortion, corruption and exploitation concealed behind a facade of colonial administration as false as the Khedive's pretensions to being a European power. Its authority was vested in venal and lazy officials and was backed by a poorly-led, demoralised army of 40,000 bayonets and a host of Bashi-Bazouk and mercenary Sudanese irregulars. Cowed, wretched and hopelessly divided, the common people of the Sudan groaned under the Egyptian yoke but were unable to see of what rotting wood it was made.

Only the Arab slavers flourished because although Egypt was officially committed to the abolition of the slave trade, its pickings were too tempting for the officials not to turn a blind eye. Of all the slavers none flourished more than the most notorious and most powerful, Zobeir Rahama, the virtually independent ruler of the Bahr-el-Ghazal, who, after routing an Egyptian force sent against him, conquered and enslaved the kingdom of Darfur and presented it to the Khedive Ismail who rewarded him with the title of Pasha.

To disarm foreign suspicion of Egypt's ambivalent attitude to the slave trade, Ismail appointed in 1874 as Governor of the Sudan's Equatorial Province a British colonel of the Royal Engineers, a man of intense religious faith, of concern for the welfare of small orphans, a highly successful leader of Chinese

Irrigation in the Sudan. A water-wheel on the Nile.

A group of riverine Sudanese of the type most exploited by Khedivial rule.

irregulars – the moody, volatile, neurotic but enormously courageous and energetic Charles George Gordon. Disgusted by what he found, depicting the Egyptian administration as 'brigandage of the very worst description', and with few resources other than his own crusading zeal, Gordon swept like a whirlwind about the Equatorial Province, chastening the lax and corrupt Egyptian officials, combating injustice and oppression wherever he found it and striking at the roots of the slave trade. Appointed Governor-General of the entire Sudan in 1877, he crushed a rebellion in the Bahr-el-Ghazal led, during Zobeir's absence in Cairo, by the slaver's son, Suleiman, who was captured and shot with eleven confederates, thus dealing a heavy blow at the iniquitous human traffic.

In 1879 Gordon left the Sudan but the departure of his authority left a vacuum which his Egyptian successor, Raouf Pasha, had neither the inclination nor the capacity to fill. With Gordon's iron grip relaxed, the Baggara perceived how feeble were the instruments that had subdued them and spoiled their trade. The Egyptian soldiers and officials, freed from Gordon's all-seeing eye and relentless will, 'revenged themselves for enforced good behaviour and paid off old scores with heavy

interest' on the inhabitants of the towns and villages along the Nile. But however cruelly the kourbash bit once again into their bowed backs, these people had been given a glimpse of justice, order and humanity which they had never experienced before, and downtrodden, debased even though they were, that glimpse had made them restive, resentful of the oppression which had returned and with an awakened hatred for the oppressors. In Gordon's wake the peoples of the Sudan began to smoulder. All that was needed was a spark to ignite them into flames.

The Islamic faith contains a latent fanaticism which, when aroused by some holy man with special gifts of striking a chord in the minds of his listeners, can impel its believers into concerted action of a most violent and self-sacrificing nature, no matter how impoverished, mentally and physically, they may have been previously; indeed the more impoverished they are, the more susceptible they become to promises of salvation. So it was in the Sudan after Gordon's departure. To work upon the minds of the harried and oppressed, to appeal to the Arab slavers embittered by and increasingly contemptuous of the foreign army which had attacked their livelihood, there came the word of one Mohammed Ahmed, a Dongolawi boat-builder's apprentice turned religious teacher. In August 1881, being then of the same age and bearing the same name as the Prophet Mohammed when he declared his mission, and with parents whose names also corresponded with those of the Prophet's, Mohammed Ahmed proclaimed himself the awaited 'Mahdi', the guide who would lead the way to true salvation. His task was to expunge the hated 'Turk' from the Sudan, and then from Egypt, and subsequently to establish Islam throughout the world, destroying any – Christian, Moslem, or pagan – who opposed him.

An attempt by Raouf Pasha to capture him at Abba Island on the White Nile failed ignominiously, two companies of Egyptian soldiers being butchered by the Mahdi's followers armed with little more than sticks and stones. The news spread throughout the Sudan as the Mahdi retreated into Kordofan where the tribes rallied to him. Outlying Egyptian posts were attacked, officials were murdered and arms were stolen. As their numbers increased the Mahdists grew bolder. In December an Egyptian force of 1400 men was ambushed and slaughtered near Fashoda. The rebellion spread into Darfur to the west and to Sennar on the Blue Nile to the east. Ill-armed and enduring great privations, the rebels had little to sustain themselves other than their faith but the Egyptians, while achieving some scattered successes, were for the most part incompetently led by men who completely under-estimated their opponents. A year after the Mahdi's emergence (while far to the north Arabi's revolt was at its height) 4000 Egyptian troops were overwhelmed by the Mahdists in southern Kordofan, as others were cut off and blockaded within their garrisons. By the end of 1882 a great sweep of land had been flooded by the Mahdist revolt, its waves lapping northwards to within 50 miles of Khartoum. Within this area a few beleaguered Egyptian garrisons still held out, the stoutest resistance being put up at El Obeid, the chief town of Kordofan, where Mohammed Pasha Said refused all calls to surrender. After six months' siege, its garrison reduced by starvation and defection to the rebels, El Obeid fell in January 1883. Some 6000 rifles and five guns with ammunition, plus £100,000, were taken by the Mahdi who set up his headquarters in the town.

Far away in Cairo urgent appeals from Khartoum for reinforcements had been received by Tewfik's ministers. But where were these to come from? Except for the Sudan garrisons, the old Egyptian Army of Arabi had been disbanded after Tel-el-Kebir and the new force then being trained by Evelyn Wood, only 6000 strong, was not ready and in any case was only for employment within Egypt proper. As far as Tewfik's British advisors were concerned, their task was to implement Gladstone's policy of setting Egypt on its feet and departing as soon as possible; the Sudan was a purely Egyptian problem with which they were not concerned and to which there was no question of sending British troops. However, since it was difficult to judge the reliability of Egyptian reports from Khartoum at such a distance, Lieutenant-Colonel Hamill Stewart of the 11th Hussars had been despatched up-river in December 1882 to report. His first message commented drily, 'The new year has begun unfavourably for Egyptian interest.'

In a desperate attempt to retain the southern provinces, Egyptian ministers hastily recalled

Charles George Gordon, Governor of the Sudan's Equatorial Province from 1874 and Governor-General of the whole Sudan from 1877–79 in his Egyptian uniform of that office. Photograph c 1880.

10,000 men of Arabi's army and sent them south, many of them in chains, accompanied by a few British officers at the Khedive's request. Among these was Colonel William Hicks, aged 52 and recently retired from the Indian Army but now promoted major-general in the Egyptian service as chief-of-staff to the 75-year-old Suliman Pasha, the nominal commander of this ill-trained, totally reluctant rabble in arms. Though grateful for the employment, Hicks had no knowledge of the Sudan or desert warfare and, apart from service in the Indian Mutiny nearly thirty years before and as a brigade-major during the Abyssinian campaign of 1868, he could only bring to this task a fine, soldierly appearance and undoubted courage. Before leaving Cairo one of his British staff was advised by brother officers to get himself a good fast horse.

On arrival at Khartoum Hicks had to spend time trying to instil some drill and discipline into the Egyptian troops, whose conduct filled Hamill Stewart with 'contempt and disgust'. The work bore fruit for it enabled Hicks to defeat some Mahdists south of Khartoum, thus temporarily pacifying the area between the White and Blue Niles. The next step was an expedition into Kordofan to recover El Obeid, but without further reinforcements and funds, and unless he was put in sole command (so impossible was the relationship with Suliman Pasha) Hicks was unwilling to set out. Eventually, after receiving confirmation of the command, though far less than he had asked for in the way of money and men both in quantity and quality, he advanced westwards into the wastes of Kordofan on 9 September 1883 with 7000 Egyptian infantry, some Bashi-Bazouk cavalry, fourteen guns, six machine-guns and no less than 2000 camp followers. Seldom, if ever, has a British officer had to undertake such a forlorn enterprise with such spiritless troops in such an undeserving cause, but for poor Hicks, with a wife and family to support, doubtless it was better to be a general active in the Egyptian Army than a retired colonel on half-pay.

For a month he spurred his unhappy fellah conscripts on into the desert. Somewhere ahead the Mahdi gathered his host together and sent scouts to watch the stumbling advance. Hicks' reports spoke of the intense heat, his anxiety about future water supplies and the uncertainty of his guides' information. On 3 October he reported that he would have to cut adrift from his line of communication and its supply dumps since their guards would simply abandon them. Loading his camels with fifty days' supplies, he advanced again. This was the last despatch to be received by those anxiously waiting at Khartoum. In the ensuing weeks rumours reached the city: that Hicks had won a victory; that he had been attacked but had repulsed the enemy; that El Obeid had fallen; that he was surrounded and short of food; that he had been ambushed and overwhelmed. By late November it seemed certain that neither Hicks nor any of his men would ever be seen again. Led astray by treacherous guides, lost and waterless, the enfeebled army had blundered into the Mahdi's trap and was massacred almost to a man, Hicks and his few European officers fighting to the last. His generalship had lost Egypt's last field army but his personal bravery remained long in the minds of his conquerors.

Fear and consternation gripped Khartoum. Four miles of defences had been prepared around the city but there were only 6000 troops to defend them. The Mahdi now had some 40,000 men under arms and had taken nearly 21,000 rifles and 19 guns since the rebellion began. Far to the west in Darfur the Austrian governor, Slatin Bey, had been holding out in a few garrisons but, on hearing of Hicks' defeat and undermined by treachery, he had been compelled to surrender. To the south, the former English merchant seaman, Lupton Bey in the Bahr-el-Ghazal and the Prussian Emin Pasha in the Equatorial Province still maintained a toehold of small garrisons but, with Mahdism supreme south of Khartoum from Darfur to Abyssinia, they were virtually cut

Lieutenant-Colonel J.D. Hamill Stewart, 11th Hussars, who was sent to report on the Sudan in 1882 and accompanied Gordon to Khartoum in 1884.

General William Hicks Pasha (seated right), the leader of the ill-fated Kordofan expedition of 1883 with members of his staff. On his right is General Valentine Baker Pasha, commander of the Egyptian Gendarmerie and of the first Egyptian expedition to Suakin in 1884.

Tribesmen of the eastern Sudan. Those with the broad-bladed swords are Hadendoa, the archetypal 'Fuzzy-Wuzzy' of Kipling.

off from the north. Nor was this all, for on the Red Sea around the port of Suakin a Turco-Hadendoa slave trader, Osman Digna, had thrown in his lot with the Mahdi and attacked the Egyptian garrisons of Sinkat and Tokar and laid siege to Suakin itself. If Suakin fell, the alternative route from Egypt to Khartoum down the Red Sea and across the desert via Berber would be lost, leaving only the Nile route which might be cut at any time.

When news of Hicks' disaster and the danger to Khartoum reached Cairo, Sir Evelyn Baring sent it on to London, pointing out that nothing could now save the Sudan and asking for instructions as to what advice he should give the Egyptian Government, for advice he was in duty bound to give by virtue of his position as the mentor of that Government. Earlier Gladstone had announced that the British army of occupation in Cairo was to be withdrawn and reduced to a small garrison at Alexandria. If British involvement in the Sudan had been out of the question at the start of the Mahdi's rebellion, even more so was it now. Baring was instructed to recommend Egypt's evacuation of the Sudan.

Reluctantly the Khedive's ministers agreed. But it is one thing to formulate a policy, quite another to effect it. How were the unfortunate men and their dependants in the remaining Egyptian garrisons – tiny, scattered islands in a vast turbulent sea of revolt – to be brought to safety? If Britain would not help, there seemed to the Egyptians only one man between the Mediterranean and the Equator with sufficient prestige, drive and ability to counter the Mahdi's influence and save the garrisons – Zobeir Pasha. To high-minded English Liberals, however, the very idea of employing an infamous slaver was shocking, but in refusing to contemplate Egypt's nominee England would have to suggest an alternative: a man of stature and experience, incorruptible, even high-minded himself, who moreover could be trusted to work a miracle at no risk and, even more important, no expense to England. There was such a man to hand, the epitome of 'the Christian hero' in Wolseley's phrase, about to take service in the Congo for the King of the Belgians. Early in December Lord Granville telegraphed to Baring to enquire whether the services of Major-General Charles Gordon might be useful.

Baring, who neither liked nor trusted Gordon, resisted strongly on the grounds that to plunge a Christian, however heroic and experienced, into a fury of Islamic fanaticism

Sir Evelyn Baring, 1st Earl of Cromer (1841–1917). Appointed to Egypt as a commissioner of the public debt in 1877, he became controller-general of finance in 1879 and was British Agent and Consul-General in Egypt from 1883–1907. Painting dated 1902 by J.S. Sargent.

would only exacerbate the situation. In this he was at first supported by the Egyptian authorities, who presumably hoped for more from Britain than one eccentric major-general. But as the days slipped by and Granville continued to urge Gordon's suitability, assuring Baring that Gordon would only be sent out to assess the situation and report back, the Egyptians changed their tune and asked for a qualified British officer to conduct the evacuation. Baring yielded, but on the understanding that Gordon would adhere strictly to the policy of a quick and early withdrawal. The telegrams giving Granville's concept of Gordon as observer, and Baring's of him as executor, crossed and consequently there was confusion over Gordon's role from the start.

As for Gordon himself, he had earlier expressed the view that evacuation was not feasible but, as Governmental pressure and public opinion built up on him to go, his religious sensibilities overcame his practical commonsense, impelling him to the Sudan in furtherance of some Divine Will. What he would actually do when he got there would depend on what he found.

On the afternoon of 18 January 1884 Gordon had his final meeting with ministers in London. Whatever the ministers may have thought they had said about confining his activities to reporting and recommending, Gordon wrote that evening to a clergyman friend to say he had agreed to go out at once and 'superintend' the evacuation. That night, accompanied by Colonel Hamill Stewart who was to go with him as, said Gordon, 'my wet-nurse', he boarded a train at Charing Cross station, dressed in 'a shabby, not to say shiny frock coat'. The Foreign Secretary bought his ticket, the Duke of Cambridge opened the carriage door, and Wolseley pressed £300 in gold into his hands, having spent the evening collecting this sum from friends in clubs after learning that his old but unworldly friend was without cash. Thus did Charles George Gordon depart on his long journey that was to end in Khartoum.

7

A Conflict of Wills

In the hope of avoiding the hotbed of intrigue and prevarication he suspected he would find in Cairo, Gordon had intended to travel direct to Khartoum via Suakin and Berber. This route was now blocked by Osman Digna's uprising which had become so serious that in December reinforcements had been sent from Cairo to Suakin. Since the Egyptian Army could not provide them, they were predominantly of the Gendarmerie under Baker Pasha. Once the highly-talented and much respected commanding officer of the 10th Hussars, he had entered the Turkish service after being found guilty of indecently assaulting a girl in a railway carriage and had distinguished himself in the Russo-Turkish War. Many had thought he should have had Evelyn Wood's job but the 7-year-old court case was still held against him (notwithstanding doubts about the verdict) and he had had to be content with the Gendarmerie who were mostly old soldiers.

Neither his courage as a man nor his skill as a commander were of any avail when, on 4 February while marching to relieve Tokar, Osman Digna's horde was sighted at El Teb. Some Turkish cavalry bolted, careered into the infantry who panicked while attempting to form square, and within no time the Hadendoa were butchering them. More than two-thirds

The landing of Baker Pasha's all-Egyptian force at Trinkitat for the relief of Tokar on 28 January 1884. Its total defeat led to the despatch of a British expedition to Suakin. Sketch for the *Illustrated London News* by the war artist, Melton Prior.

were lost. After vainly trying to rally the terrified troops, Baker managed to embark the survivors at Trinkitat and return to Suakin. Four days later the garrison at Sinkat was also destroyed.

It was clear that if an evacuation of the Sudan was to stand a chance Suakin must be held, but that it would not be done by Egyptian troops. In London Wolseley urged upon the Secretary for War, Lord Hartington, the necessity of using British troops. There was already a Royal Navy squadron off-shore under Admiral Hewett who, on 10 February, landed marines and took over Suakin. Two days later General Stephenson, commanding in Cairo, was ordered to send a force[3] from Egypt under Major-General Graham, which was to be joined by other troops[4] then on their way home from India, to drive away Osman Digna.

After a proclamation bidding the Arabs disperse had been ignored, Graham advanced on 29 February against Osman Digna's position at El Teb where the slaver had entrenched his riflemen with the Krupp guns taken from Baker. Graham formed his five battalions and Royal Marines into a square, or rather rectangle, with his eight 7-pounders and six Gatlings at the corners, and marched against the enemy left to roll up the position from a flank. The Arabs resisted fiercely with musketry and shrapnel and, once their guns were silenced, by headlong charges with spear and sword against the advancing square. Despite the enemy's fearless attacks, the disciplined infantry pushed on, gradually clearing the trenches and rifle-pits. Seeing some of the enemy giving way, Brigadier-General Herbert Stewart led the 10th and 19th Hussars in a charge, but in the course of it they by-passed a large body of Arabs concealed in the scrub. These leaped up to attack the rear squadrons. Wheeling about, the two regiments reformed and charged again but the thorn scrub broke up their formation. Small groups and individuals found themselves assailed by men

who seemed to appear out of the ground, hamstringing the horses and spearing the riders, who found it difficult to sabre men lying on the ground stabbing upwards. Colonel Barrow of the 19th was surrounded and severely wounded, and must have been killed had not Quartermaster-Sergeant Marshall galloped up with a spare horse and rescued him; Marshall was later awarded the Victoria Cross. Several charges were made, but not until some of the troopers were dismounted to open fire with their carbines did the cavalry begin to gain the upper hand. Even so the 10th and 19th lost twenty killed and forty-eight wounded, in contrast with the infantry and artillery losses of ten killed and ninety-four wounded.

Severe casualties had been inflicted on the Hadendoa and their allies, most of whom held their ground to the last, but a second summons to submit again received a defiant reply. Accordingly Graham, having concentrated his force at Suakin, determined to strike at Osman's camp around the wells of Tamai.

On the morning of 13 March, cavalry scouts having reported only scattered groups of enemy in front, Graham attacked Tamai with his infantry formed in two brigade squares, one echeloned back 1000 yards to the right rear of the other. As the leading square – 1st Black Watch, 1st York and Lancaster and a Naval Brigade – approached the edge of a ravine, a great mass of Hadendoa surged up out of it and hurled themselves at the infantry. The square immediately halted and opened fire but so fierce and rapid was the onset that the York and Lancasters were forced back. Blinded by the smoke and dust and deafened by the noise, the desperately fighting men could not hear the shouted commands. A machine-gun jammed and a gap opened between the front and flank sides of the square into which the Arabs poured. The orderly formation dissolved into a confused mass of savage hand-to-hand fighting, bayonet against sword and spear. The Black Watch had at least seen action at Tel-el-Kebir but for the York and Lancasters, straight from a peaceful garrison in India, it was a new and terrifying experience to face waves of bounding, leaping tribesmen, turning the bayonets

---

[3] 19th Hussars; 1st Black Watch, 1st Gordon Highlanders, 3rd King's Royal Rifle Corps.
[4] 10th Hussars; 1st York and Lancaster, 2nd Royal Irish Fusiliers. (The 2nd and 1st Battalions of these two regiments had returned to England after Tel-el-Kebir.)

The charge of the 10th (Prince of Wales's Own Royal) Hussars at the Battle of El Teb, 29 February 1884. The Regiment fought in Indian khaki drill frocks with blue pantaloons and puttees. Painting by Major G.D. Giles, Bombay Staff Corps, who was present during the campaign.

with their shields and slashing with their long, double-edged swords. The machine-guns were overrun, their Naval crews hacked down, but the heroic lone fight by Private Edwards of the Black Watch to save the mules carrying the guns' ammunition was to win him the Victoria Cross. Though the infantry fought on as best they could in the shambles of the square, all would have been lost but for the arrival of the other brigade.

Commanded by the brave and imperturbable Redvers Buller, the 3rd KRRC, 1st Gordons and 2nd Royal Irish Fusiliers had opened fire as soon as the attack began. Being at a greater distance from the ravine, they had more time and a good field of fire for their controlled volleys to take effect on the Arabs' left thrust which, failing to reach Buller's men, swung right to pile into the broken square. Seeing the dangerous plight of the embattled forward brigade, Buller advanced to come up on its right, while Stewart ordered part of his cavalry to gallop forward

round the left, dismount and open fire on the enemy right. This combined supporting fire from the flanks enabled the leading square to rally and reform.

Though Osman's men still swarmed forward with fanatical bravery, the British volleys now took a terrible toll. With both brigades holding firm on the lip of the ravine, it became clear to Osman that spears and swords, however bravely wielded, would not prevail further against rifles, machine-guns and artillery. He drew off his followers, not in flight but in a sullen and reluctant retreat, leaving some 2000 of his dead and many wounded who, despite their injuries, still showed fight as Buller's brigade advanced to clear the battlefield and burn the camp. In nearly three hours of intense fighting 109 British officers and men had been killed and another 112 wounded.

Graham had wished to follow up this action by pushing Stewart forward towards Berber, a bold but risky move favoured by Gordon who, having arrived at Khartoum on 18 February, had been concerned about news of a possible uprising at Shendi, south of Berber, which could interrupt communications down the Nile from Khartoum. However Whitehall refused to countenance any further operations in the eastern Sudan and in late March ordered Graham to withdraw, leaving a small garrison to hold Suakin itself.

Graham had dealt two heavy blows at Osman Digna but had only compelled him to retreat, not submit. Furthermore the operations had done nothing to assist Gordon's position at Khartoum for the Mahdists had attacked at Shendi as forecast, cutting the telegraph between Khartoum and Berber. Gordon's communications now depended on his river steamers being able to get through to Berber which was still in Egyptian hands.

If nothing else this interruption to Gordon's communications afforded some respite to Baring in Cairo who, since Gordon's arrival, had been bombarded by a barrage of telegrams from Khartoum, the outpourings of the envoy's fertile mind as he devised solution after solution for the task he believed had been laid upon him. Given a rapturous welcome by the people of Khartoum, Gordon set out to stiffen their resolve and wean them from any ideas of adherence to the Mahdi by removing the worst abuses of Egyptian rule and by offering them more than they could hope to gain from 'the false prophet'. He improved the food supply, set free prisoners who had been held without trial, and destroyed the Egyptian officials' debt records and torture instruments; most popular of all he halved the taxes and permitted slavery to continue. He made no secret of the fact that he had come to evacuate all the Egyptian troops and officials, an honest but unwise announcement, that caused misgivings among the merchant class who feared the Mahdi, as shortly afterwards it was to induce the Sudanese nota-

bles at Berber to defect to him. Measures to begin the evacuation were put in hand. At the same time Gordon concerned himself with the vacuum which would ensue during and after the withdrawal of the Egyptian administration, and which would inevitably be filled by the Mahdi unless some better system of government could be devised. It was clear to Gordon and, after persuasion, to Hamill Stewart and Baring, that the only man with sufficient ability who would be acceptable to the Sudan was Zobeir Pasha. But however suitable Zobeir may have appeared to the necessarily pragmatic men on the spot, his notorious reputation – particularly after Gordon's surprising condonation of his profession – again caused a shudder of revulsion in London and a stiff refusal followed. Pressed by Gordon, Baring continued to urge upon the Government the necessity for Zobeir but to no avail. The final dashing of Gordon's hopes never reached him for by then the telegraph was cut, and the Mahdists were closing in on Khartoum from the north, the south-west and the south-east.

The town, a conglomeration of dirty white houses topped by the minaret of a mosque, was set upon a barren strip of land on the left bank of the Blue Nile about a mile above its confluence with the White Nile. Its population fluctuated around 50,000, of which some two-thirds were negro slaves, and about 12,000 were non-Sudanese – Egyptians, Syrians, Copts, Turks and Greeks. The town was protected on three sides by the two Niles while the open approaches to the south-east were guarded by an eight-foot-deep ditch and a rampart which stretched for some four miles between the river banks. The ditch and ground forward of it were sown with broken bottles, spear-heads, spiked iron balls and electrically-detonated mines made out of biscuit boxes. On the right and left banks of the Blue and White Niles respectively were two outlying forts, the North Fort and Omdurman. To defend this long perimeter Gordon had some 6000 Egyptian regulars and Bashi-Bazouks, of which the most reliable were 2400 black Sudanese troops, and about 3000 irregulars and volunteers. A vital asset of the defence were the seven river steamers which

THEATRE OF OPERATIONS IN THE SUDAN, 1883–99 (see also map on p. 123)

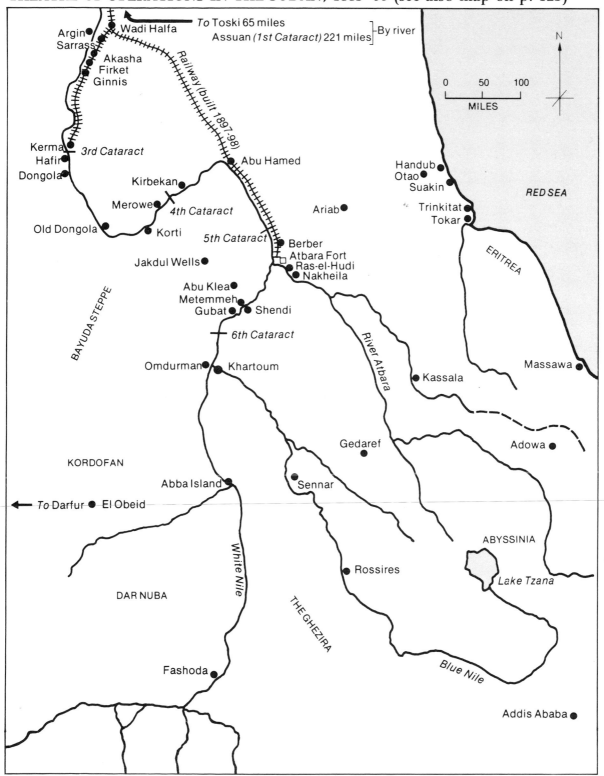

THE MAHDI'S REBELLION

The Battle of Tamai, 13 March 1884. Osman Digna's Hadendoa attacking Graham's leading square. Painting by G.D. Giles.

Inside the square of the 1st Black Watch and 1st York and Lancaster at Tamai as the Hadendoa attack. The Highlanders were in grey frocks and kilts, the English battalion in Indian khaki drill. The latter still had the outdated pouch-belt equipment. Painting by G.D. Giles.

Stewart had armed with cannon and machine-guns. Though the troops and many of their officers were of doubtful quality, there was at least no shortage of ammunition and food stocks sufficient for six months.

By the time Gordon's communications were cut in mid-March, he had only succeeded in evacuating some 2000 civilians and sick soldiers. There was nothing he could do for the remaining garrisons south and east of Khartoum who would have to try to reach Central Africa, Abyssinia or Suakin. Gordon's concern was therefore with Khartoum itself but, as the Mahdist cordon closed in, the chances of getting any large numbers away down the Nile disappeared, particularly as Gordon felt as much responsibility for the non-Sudanese civilians as for the soldiers, officials and their families. It was true that a steamer or two could probably get through, but with the town under fire, with the Mahdists across the Nile to the north and all his requests and recommendations to London ignored or refused, Gordon perceived that his responsibilities now crystallised into a single, clear task: the protection of the people of Khartoum from the fanatical hordes of the Mahdi until help could reach him. To this end he thenceforth applied all his courage, ingenuity and leadership.

Baring, realising Gordon's and Stewart's dangerous position and anticipating that they would not leave Khartoum to its fate, telegraphed to the Cabinet urging that, if help could not be sent immediately, at least an expedition should be despatched in the autumn, reminding ministers that 'it is our bounden duty not to abandon him.' In similar vein the Queen wrote imperiously to Gladstone, 'You are bound to try and save him.' To these and other exhortations which grew in volume and number as the weeks passed, Gladstone remained impervious. He had agreed reluctantly to the Egyptian expedition of 1882 and to Graham's rescue of Suakin, but he had forbidden the advance to Berber and was in no mind for further military adventures when there were more pressing domestic matters, of greater concern to the realm as he saw it, than the possible but by no means certain fate of one headstrong and erratic

major-general. He procrastinated, claiming that Gordon had exceeded his brief, that he could get away any time, that the situation had been misrepresented, that there was insufficient justification for an expedition. As spring passed into summer, as the danger to Khartoum worsened – Berber falling to the Mahdi in May – so the pressure to rescue Gordon increased, from the Court, the Opposition, public opinion, from members of Gladstone's own party, even within the Cabinet. In the latter the chief protagonists for an expedition were the Radicals, Dilke and Chamberlain, and the War Secretary, Lord Hartington, who not only felt an obligation towards Gordon but also had to contend with Wolseley ever at his ear, urging the need for action.

In April Wolseley had submitted memoranda which outlined a requirement for a relief force, entirely British, of 6500 men and the preparations which would be necessary if Gordon was to be reached before 15 November, beyond which he did not think Khartoum could hold out. The routes such a force should take provoked great argument, chiefly between the merits of Suakin – Berber across the desert and Wadi Halfa – Berber up the Nile. The former was much shorter but posed water problems (not to mention the hostile Hadendoa outside Suakin) and would require the construction of a railway; while the lengthy passage of the Nile would be upstream against the hazardous cataracts. Wolseley himself preferred the Nile route, basing his choice on his highly successful Red River Expedition in Canada in 1870. Generals Stephenson and Wood in Cairo, on the other hand, pronounced against it on the grounds of distance, logistics and the cataracts. The fall of Berber in May seriously weakened the case for the desert route, but the argument raged on through the summer, culminating in a Royal Naval report that the Nile route was impracticable for small boats. Unimpressed, Wolseley countered with a contrary paper prepared by officers who had been with him on the Red River – but had no experience of the Upper Nile.

All this increasingly heated argument in Parliament and among the military was grist to

Sailors with Gardner machine-guns in the eastern Sudan.
Drawing by A. Forestier. This was the type of gun that jammed
at Tamai.

Model of Gordon's palace at Khartoum, as reconstructed by W.
Holmes FRSA in c 1900. The far side of the main building
abutted on to the left bank of the Blue Nile, the front faced into
the town and trees surrounded the flanking walls.

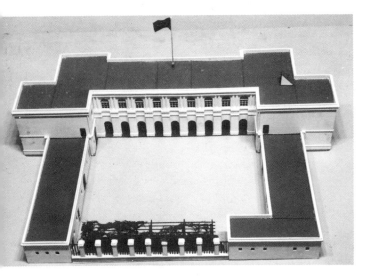

Gladstone's mill, enabling him to delay and
temporise. The greater the uproar on behalf of
Gordon – the public hissing and booing, the
white feathers – the more obdurate he became.
No more British blood and treasure would he
expend in the desert sand 'in a war of conquest
against a people struggling, and rightly struggling, to be free'; certainly not to rescue one
man whose predicament was of his own choos-
ing. Over 2000 miles away that man was equally

stubborn, refusing, in the name of honour, to
abandon the frightened and imperilled people
in his charge. In the summer of 1884 the fighting in the Sudan, the bitter arguments at home
were all secondary to the conflict between the
wills of these two men, each convinced of his
own rectitude.

Once Berber had fallen and the Mahdists
tightened the noose around Khartoum, such
messages as Gordon was able to smuggle out or
have secreted in could take months in their
transmission, if they got through at all, so that
their contents were over-taken by events –
something Gladstone seemed unable or unwilling to appreciate. As the weeks sped past and
still nothing was done for Gordon, the Cabinet
minister most unhappy with Gladstone's stone-
walling was Hartington. Though indecisive, he
was nevertheless respected both for his integ-
rity and as head of the aristocratic Whig element in the Liberal Party. In June, alarmed for
the safety of Egypt itself, he had authorised
General Stephenson to despatch two British
battalions to Assuan and Keneh as a back-up to
Wood's Egyptian troops on the frontier at Wadi
Halfa. On 20 July the first message from Gordon
for three months was received, dated a month
before and stating that Khartoum was holding
out but asking where the relief expedition was.
When Gladstone yet again sought refuge in
some unhelpful, non-committal reply, Hartington's long-suppressed conscience drove him to
threaten resignation unless an expedition were
sent. 'It is a question of personal honour and

Bank-notes issued by Gordon during the siege of Khartoum.
Each bears his signature and is franked with a stamp bearing
the Egyptian star and crescent and the legend 'Gouvernorat
Général du Soudan'.

Decoration for gallantry instituted by Gordon at Khartoum.
There were three classes: pewter (illustrated here), silver and
gold. The central device was originally a grenade.

good faith and I do not see how I can yield upon
it.' Such sentiments cut no ice with Gladstone
but Hartington's resignation would have
brought down the Government. Grudgingly,
qualifying every concession, Gladstone had to
yield, moving in Parliament on 5 August, for a
credit of £300,000 towards 'operations for the
relief of General Gordon, should they become
necessary.'

Throughout August Gladstone continued to
persuade himself that no expedition would be
needed, still employing every delaying tactic he
could to prevent it. Had he but known it, there
was evidence to buttress his arguments in
Khartoum itself at the very time of Hartington's
ultimatum. Gordon's policy of conducting an
aggressive defence using his steamers had
scored two signal successes over his besiegers,
enabling him to report to Baring that Khartoum
was in good heart and that he was making plans

to recapture Berber. However Baring did not
receive this message until the end of September
by which time the situation had deteriorated.
On 4 September Gordon had sent nearly a
thousand of his best troops under his most
reliable commander to break up an enemy force
on the Blue Nile. The rebels were routed, but in
pursuing them Gordon's men went beyond the
range of their steamers' guns, fell into an
ambush and were destroyed. This was a serious
blow both in loss of men and munitions, and to
the morale of Khartoum, which the Mahdists
now invested more closely. Worse was to
follow.

Desperate to appraise the outside world of
Khartoum's plight and its need for help, Gordon
decided to send Hamill Stewart down the Nile
to try and reach the nearest telegraph at
Dongola. Stewart was reluctant to leave Gordon
on his own but agreed. Accompanied by the

Lieutenant-Colonel Hon. R. Talbot, 1st Life Guards, commanding the Heavy Camel Regiment composed of detachments from
the Household Cavalry, Dragoon Guards, Dragoon and Lancer
regiments.

Lieutenant-Colonel Hon. E.E. Boscawen, Coldstream Guards,
commanding the Guards Camel Regiment, composed of
detachments from the Grenadier, Coldstream and Scots Guards
and Royal Marines.

only other Englishman in Khartoum, Frank
Power of *The Times*, and the French Consul,
Stewart set off in the steamer *Abbas* on 8
September. They ran the gauntlet of Shendi and
Berber successfully but some miles beyond the
Abbas went aground in a cataract. Offered shel-
ter by a local sheik, Stewart and his companions
landed and were all murdered. Gordon would
not learn of this tragedy for some time so could
not know that his message had failed to get
through. Moreover, now that he was deprived

of Stewart's sterling qualities and company, the
daily anxiety of directing and rallying the
doubtful soldiery and polyglot population was
henceforth his alone. The Mahdi's main army
with artillery had reinforced the besiegers, but
for Gordon — his supplies and ammunition di-
minishing, his troops kept to their duty by fear
of the consequences and his promises of relief —
there was only his journal to confide in, his
religious faith to sustain him and the hope that
his country would not let him down.

Though Gordon was mercifully unaware of it there had, hitherto, been every indication that such hope, resting as it did on Gladstone, was grievously misplaced: but on the day after Stewart had left Khartoum on his fatal voyage, Wolseley had arrived in Cairo, charged with the command of a relief expedition. He had got his way over the routes and his army was to assemble at the railhead of Sarrass, just south of Wadi Halfa, there to proceed in boats, or whalers, up the Nile to Dongola, a distance of 234 miles and, if necessary, on to Khartoum – nearly another 600 miles – a passage which would have to negotiate four of the Nile's six major cataracts. To this end 800 whalers were even then being constructed in England under the supervision of Colonel Butler, a veteran of the Red River Expedition. Experienced boatmen to pilot them were being summoned from Canada, West Africa and Aden. The force, a cavalry regiment, a mountain battery and eight battalions, some 6000 men in all, was to be drawn from the British troops stationed in Egypt. However, so great were the distances and so hazardous the enterprise, not to mention the time already lost and the time it would take to get the expedition under way, that Wolseley urged the immediate formation of a small flying column, to be mounted on camels and drawn from picked volunteers of the Army's élite regiments at home, the Household and Line Cavalry, the Foot Guards and Rifles. Despite a furious protest from the Duke of Cambridge at what he saw as another of Wolseley's attacks on regimental *esprit de corps*, the Camel Corps was rapidly formed, a roll of its officers reading like pages from *Debrett* – fifteen of them having titles. On 26 September it sailed for Egypt. There was still a mass of preparations to be made: medical arrangements, the collection of stores and supplies, the purchase of camels, the transportation of the whalers, the movement of troops south. But at last, six months after Gordon had been cut off, help was on the way. The question was, would they be in time?

8

Against Nature and Time

Wolseley hoped that the appearance of his force in the region of Dongola, even knowledge of its approach, might cause the Mahdists to waver in their resolve and disperse. His mission was the relief of Gordon, not the defeat of the Mahdi, though it would become increasingly clear that the former could not be accomplished without fighting. Moreover, as the campaign's official historian has pointed out, 'the Nile expedition was a campaign less against man, than against nature and against time.' Although the Nile would water the force, its currents and cataracts would delay it, while the desert on either side could offer no resources whatever. Therefore everything necessary for the maintenance of troops and animals would first have to be collected in Egypt and then transported up the river with the fighting troops, with consequent overloading and slowing down of the limited numbers of boats and camels available. All would conspire to eat up precious time, so much of which had already been lost in London.

Nor was the need for speed assisted by the system which organised the arrangements. It was symbolic of the amateur approach of the Victorian Army that the transportation of the troops, their boats and supplies to the jumping-off point of Wadi Halfa had to be entrusted to Thomas Cook and Sons. Skilled they may have been at ferrying tourists up and down the Lower Nile but through misunderstandings and a lack of military staff supervision, their steamers ran out of coal at a crucial period of the build-up at Wadi Halfa with an ensuing delay of thirteen days. For a commander's staff to implement efficiently his orders, it must contain trained staff officers working to a tried and uniform system. Wolseley's senior subordinates were hastily-assembled members of his famous 'Ring' – Buller, Herbert Stewart, Brackenbury, Butler and others. All were able

officers who had achieved distinction in the field, though not necessarily in the type of appointments they were now given. For example, Buller had earned Wolseley's esteem, not so much as a staff officer, but chiefly as a commander of irregular horse in the Zulu War, winning the Victoria Cross for his bravery and leadership, and lately of a brigade at Suakin, which did not necessarily qualify him for his important post on the Nile as Wolseley's Chief of Staff. Herbert Stewart, a dashing and capable dragoon and, in Wolseley's view, 'a first-rate officer all round', had led the cavalry into Cairo in 1882 and Graham's mounted troops at Suakin, but neither he nor the others had experience of the Upper Nile. The only man with wide local knowledge was Colonel Sir Charles Wilson, an experienced staff officer but not one of the Ring, who was appointed Chief of Intelligence. These men, admirable though they were individually, worked not to a universally recognised staff system – which did not then exist in the Army – but on an *ad hoc* basis according to their own abilities and temperaments; nor did they work well as a team for all were ambitious and jealous of each other. Furthermore, their personal respect for, and loyalty towards, Wolseley inhibited them from taking decisions, so that problems had to await his ruling which, over the great distances of the Nile, would be at best time-consuming and at worst impossible.

There were other factors, too, which caused delays. The railway facilities to Wadi Halfa were inadequate and in disrepair. The for-

Sir Herbert Stewart, commander of the Desert Column for the relief of Gordon. He served with distinction as a staff officer in the Zulu, Transvaal and Egyptian wars and commanded the cavalry brigade at El Teb and Tamai. He is pictured in the undress uniform of the 3rd Dragoon Guards.

16th (The Queen's) Lancers detachment of the Heavy Camel Regiment in Egypt before marching south. Seated centre front is Major T. Davison, commanding, and at each end of the rear rank is Lieutenant W.B. Browne (left) and (right) Captain Lord St Vincent, Adjutant of the Heavies and killed at Abu Klea.

mation of the Camel Corps would add another 2000 to be fed, with additional transport needed for their rations and forage. The riding and baggage camels had to be procured and saddles manufactured, and the soldiers taught to ride them. Private Etherington of the Royal Sussex recalled that the camels were 'nearly all of them diseased and swarming with maggots, while the stench was simply unbearable' and that 'learning to ride them was no treat either. I was no sooner on than I was off, and that was the case with most of us.' Butler got the whalers built in England and landed at Alexandria in just over two months, but the Canadian boatmen, laboriously brought across the Atlantic, proved not to be of the same breed as the by-then largely extinct *voyageurs*, whom Wolseley remembered from the old Red River days, but lumbermen, Red Indians and a number of city dwellers, including eight lawyers, all under a Toronto alderman. Some would render invaluable service in the boats, even volunteering to remain with the expedition after their initial contracts had expired, but others were quite unsuitable or inexperienced, while few had any knowledge of sailing. Though generally hardworking, their rough-and-ready manner did not accord with the disciplined obedience of the regular soldier. Further discord on the river arose from the conflicting ideas of the impulsive and dogmatic Butler and Lord Charles Beresford, Wolseley's highly-regarded Naval ADC. To make matters worse the Nile was falling, and in addition to the numbered cataracts, each a long series of rapids, there were others which were quite uncharted.

It was not until 6 November, three months after the expedition had been approved, that the first boat-borne battalion, 1st South Staffordshire, embarked in its whalers from the railhead and began the long pull south, followed by the other battalions in turn, though the first of these would be unable to leave before the 11th owing to the coal shortage in

Cook's steamers, and the last would not get away until 19 December. Wolseley had already joined Herbert Stewart at Dongola, which the latter had occupied with the 1st Royal Sussex as early as 29 September but, consumed with frustration at the slow progress, he rode all the way back to Wadi Halfa to discover the cause of the delay and spur Buller and Butler to greater efforts, even offering a prize of £100 to the battalion which made the best speed south – subsequently awarded to the 1st Royal Irish

which took thirty-eight days. His anxiety had been exacerbated by his ignorance of Gordon's situation and was further increased on 17 November by the first letter to reach him from Khartoum. Dated thirteen days before, Gordon wrote that five steamers had gone down to Metemmeh to await the relief column and 'we can hold out forty days with ease, after that it will be difficult.' Wolseley thereupon changed the concentration area from Dongola to Korti, near the base of the great southerly bend of the Nile between Dongola and Abu Hamed; from there the advance could continue up-river or across the desert to Metemmeh.

The Camel Corps meanwhile had been formed into four regiments: Heavy (Household Cavalry, Dragoons and Lancers), Light (Hussars), Guards (with a fourth company of Royal Marines) and Mounted Infantry (Rifles and detachments of regiments in Egypt). Six days after the Staffords, the Guards Camel Regiment led off from Wadi Halfa, following the left bank of the river. For the soldiers sweating at the oars of their unfamiliar boats and the guardsmen lurching along on their equally unfamiliar camels it was a long, hot journey of some 360 miles, though far more strenuous and difficult for the former. The Guards halted at Dongola, to await and train with the Mounted Infantry, then both camel regiments moved on to Korti, arriving there on 14 December – the last of Gordon's forty days – while the Staffords came in three days later. By this time Wolseley had received alarming reports of Gordon's failing supplies. The rest of the Camel Corps were coming on, plus part of the 19th Hussars (on horses), but no more infantry would arrive until the turn of the year and it was clear that the bulk of the River Column could not be concentrated until 22 January. Wolseley decided the moment he had envisaged when forming the Camel Corps had come.

On the assumption, based on Gordon's assurances, that the appearance before Khartoum of even a small body of British soldiers, preferably

An officer of the Guards Camel Regiment, Lieutenant B. Baden-Powell, Scots Guards.

dressed in red, would cause the break-up of the besieging Mahdists, he planned to launch his mounted troops under Herbert Stewart across the 176 miles of desert to Metemmeh, from where a picked force of 'the finest men in our or any other Army' could make the final 96-mile dash to the beleaguered Gordon. At the same time Major-General Earle was to press on up the Nile with four battalions in boats, part of the 19th Hussars and some Egyptian camel troops and guns; he was to capture Berber and move on to Shendi, opposite Metemmeh, to establish a base from which Stewart's force could be re-supplied.

The success of what Wolseley called the Desert Column's 'great leap in the dark' depended on speed and surprise. This was endangered even before the advance began when it became apparent, such was the shortage of camels to carry supplies, that Stewart, instead of advancing in one bound with all his force, would have first to establish a forward supply base at Jakdul Wells, some ninety miles from Korti, using the camels of the Heavy and Light Regiments as transport, and then return to Korti for the balance of his force.

The River Column, led by the South Staffords, set off on 28 December and on the 30th Stewart's convoy rode out into the desert, protected by the Guards and Mounted Infantry and accompanied by a camel-borne Royal Artillery battery and detachments of Royal Engineers, commissariat and medical troops. Stewart reached Jakdul without incident, unloaded and having left the Guards as garrison was back at Korti on 5 January, only to find that in his absence plans had changed again.

On the last day of 1884 Wolseley had received the first news he had had from Gordon since the latter's despatch of 4 November. A messenger brought in a piece of paper the size of a postage stamp on which was written 'Khartoum all right. 14.12.84. C.G. Gordon.', but he also delivered a verbal message: that Khartoum was besieged on three sides, with fighting going on day and night, but that the town could only fall through lack of provisions which were in short supply; that Wolseley should come quickly and in strength for the enemy were numerous; and that he should

come via Metemmeh or Berber but should not leave the latter untaken in his rear.

This news overturned the assumptions on which Wolseley's plans had been based as it now appeared too risky both to divide his force and to attempt to reach Khartoum before Berber was captured. He therefore decided to adhere to his plan for sending the Desert Column to Metemmeh but once there it was to fortify a post and, by means of Gordon's steamers which should be awaiting its arrival, communicate with Gordon to discover his situation. Meanwhile Earle was to capture Berber and, having garrisoned it with a battalion, was to push on with the rest of the River Column to link up with the Desert Column at Metemmeh. The combined force would then advance on Khartoum. Wolseley realised that this would greatly postpone Gordon's relief but, as he wrote in his journal, he intended if at any moment 'Gordon sends to tell me he is *in extremis*, to push on with all the camel regiments to Khartoum. The risk would perhaps be great, but no risk would be too great under those circumstances.'

On 8 January, Stewart set out to rejoin the Guards at Jakdul Wells, taking with him the Heavy and Mounted Infantry Camel Regiments, a squadron of the 19th Hussars, 400 men of the 1st Royal Sussex and a company of the 2nd Essex, which was to provide garrisons at vital points along his route, together with more supplies. The Light Camel Regiment found that its role was to be confined to convoy escorts and communications duties due to its commander, Colonel Stanley Clarke, a crony of the Prince of Wales, having already fallen foul of Wolseley who considered him 'worse than useless'. Accompanying Stewart as the designated commander at Metemmeh was the celebrated soldier, adventurer and traveller, Colonel Fred Burnaby of the Blues, a thorn in the side of the Duke of Cambridge who had refused Wolseley's request for his services. Not to be denied, Burnaby applied for leave to visit the Cape and joined the expedition unofficially, another instance of the eccentric workings of the Victorian military system. Also with the column was Colonel Wilson, the intelligence chief, who

KHARTOUM IN 1884-85

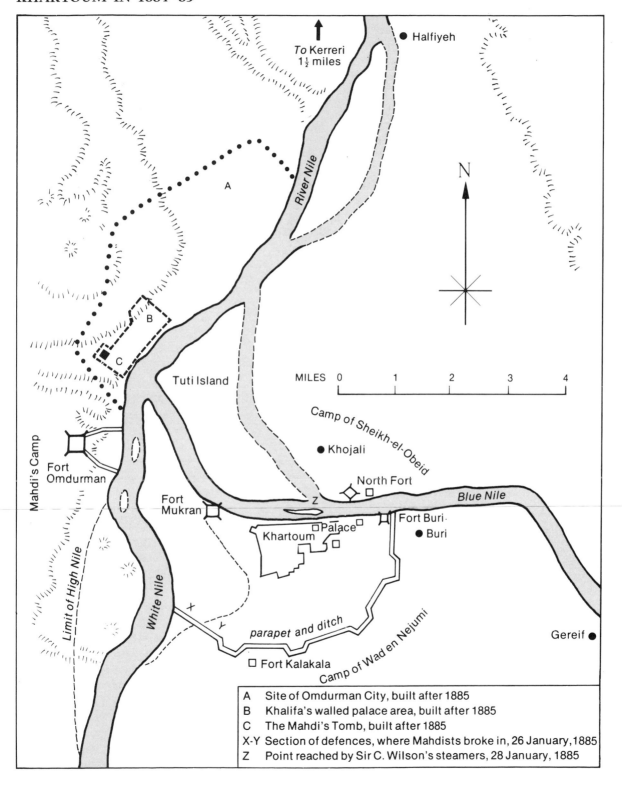

To Kerreri 1½ miles

● Halfiyeh

River Nile

N

A

B

C

Tuti Island

MILES 0   1   2   3   4

Camp of Sheikh-el-Obeid

● Khojali

North Fort

Blue Nile

Mahdi's Camp

Fort Omdurman

Fort Mukran

Z

Palace

Fort Buri

Khartoum

● Buri

Limit of High Nile

White Nile

X

Y

parapet and ditch

Camp of Wad en Nejumi

Gereif ●

□ Fort Kalakala

A   Site of Omdurman City, built after 1885
B   Khalifa's walled palace area, built after 1885
C   The Mahdi's Tomb, built after 1885
X-Y Section of defences, where Mahdists broke in, 26 January, 1885
Z   Point reached by Sir C. Wilson's steamers, 28 January, 1885

The Desert Column on the march, making 'an almost in-describably grand effect' in their grey frocks, Bedford cord breeches and blue puttees. White helmets and belts were usually stained brown.

was to contact Gordon, and Lord Charles Beresford with a 57-strong Naval Brigade which was to man the steamers at Metemmeh.

Meanwhile at Khartoum Gordon was more concerned by the lack of news of the relief column and the rapidly deteriorating food supply than the incessant long-range fire of the besiegers. On 25 November he had heard that Wolseley was no nearer than Korti but continued to encourage his people with heartening news of approaching rescue. In the evenings his small bugle-band played from the Palace roof to keep up morale and taunt the enemy, the buglers exchanging their instruments for rifles when the Mahdists responded with fire. Within the town and at its defences little escaped the gaze of his compelling blue eyes which 'seemed to possess a magic power over all who came within its influence'. He had not the troops to risk more sorties but his gunboats were frequently in action, particularly in support of the outlying fort of Omdurman on the west bank of the White Nile whose retention was vital to the safety of Khartoum itself. But Gordon's chief worry was food. On 14 December – the date of his last message to Wolseley – there only remained two weeks' supply. On the same day he concluded his journal with the words, 'If the Expeditionary Force, and I ask for no more than two hundred men, does not come in ten days, the town may fall; and I have done my best for the honour of our country. Goodbye. C.G. Gordon.' The next day he had despatched his journal and some farewell letters down-river on the steamer *Bordein*.

Somehow the remaining supplies were eked out a little longer, a small concealed store of grain was discovered, dogs were hunted in the streets, makeshift bread was made up from palm-tree cores, but by early January people were dying of hunger and many of the soldiers were too weak to carry their rifles. If Khartoum just kept going on rats and scraps of goatskin water-bags, the defenders of Omdurman were without any food at all. On or about 12 January Gordon authorised its heroic commander, Faragh Allah, to surrender. The end could not now be long delayed but daily the indomitable Gordon assured his famished and fearful followers that help was at hand, though the view from the Palace roof yielded no sign of the smoke of his returning steamers, packed with the redcoats which he yet believed might tilt the scales in his favour.

The relief force, however, had hard times ahead. After watering and grazing his by now undernourished and overworked camels at Jakdul, Stewart continued his march on 14 January, taking on the Guards and leaving as garrison of the wells 150 men of the Royal Sussex. Except for the 19th Hussars, scouting ahead on wiry little Syrian stallions, and Beresford on a white donkey, the whole column, Guards, Heavies, Mounted Infantry, Sussex, gunners and sailors were all mounted on camels riding forty abreast. Other than a hundred-odd native camel drivers, Stewart disposed of just under 1400 fighting men and 45 medical and commissariat staff. Loaded on nine camels were the Royal Artillery's three 7-pounder screw guns and 300 rounds of ammunition, while four more camels carried the sailors' Gardner gun and its 1000 rounds; this five-barrelled gun could fire at a rate of 400 rounds per minute but was grievously prone to jamming and indeed it was this very same weapon that had jammed at a critical moment at Tamai ten months before. The rest of the camel-borne troops were armed with the Martini-Henry rifle and 22-inch, wavy-bladed sword bayonet. This breech-loading rifle fired a heavy .45-inch bullet, effective against a charging, fanatical tribesman, but had a powerful recoil, took about five seconds to reload after each shot, and was also liable to jam – dangerous defects if the approaching warrior got within close range. The quality of the bayonet's steel had already caused concern at El Teb and Tamai and was later to be the subject of Parliamentary questions. Moreover the men of the Heavies were inexperienced with the rifle and bayonet, being trained to the sword or lance, and occasionally the carbine.[5] Nevertheless, the camel

regiments were filled with steady, proficient soldiers, mature men not boys and, as the column advanced across the undulating, gravelly desert, a war correspondent thought 'the height of the camels, their red saddles, and stalwart riders clad in light grey and wearing white helmets, produced an almost indescribably grand effect'.[6]

On the afternoon of the second day's march, the scouts reported many horse-tracks and traces of recent camp-fires. On the next day Stewart planned to reach the wells of Abu Klea, which lay beyond a low range of hills. During the morning the Hussars began to catch sight of small bodies of Arabs ahead. While attempting to seize a prisoner a detachment led by Major John French[7] was nearly surrounded by a large group of enemy and had to ride hard to escape. It was soon evident that the Mahdists, alerted by the convoys moving between Korti and Jakdul, had divined Stewart's intentions and were preparing to dispute his further advance. By the time Colonel Barrow, commanding the Hussars, had reported and Stewart himself had ridden forward to reconnoitre, it was after midday and large numbers of the enemy with their battle flags were massing on the hills astride the pass leading to the wells. Acutely conscious of the need to replenish his water supplies, Stewart at first intended to attack at once and ordered the main body forward and off the track, but later, realising there were only three hours of daylight left, he decided to wait till morning. The column halted on an area of level ground and enclosed itself for the night within a low rampart, or zariba, built up from the stones, rocks and thorn scrub scattered about. Rocks were in somewhat short supply so that by nightfall the wall was only two feet high and the rearmost part of the bivouac had to be protected by piled camel saddles and stores

---

[5] Most cavalry regiments at this period were reluctant to devote much time to musketry practice.

[6] The Camel Corps had been specially served out with grey serge frocks (jackets), Bedford cord pantaloons and dark blue puttees. The helmets were mostly stained brown.

[7] Later Field-Marshal and commander of the British Expeditionary Force in 1914.

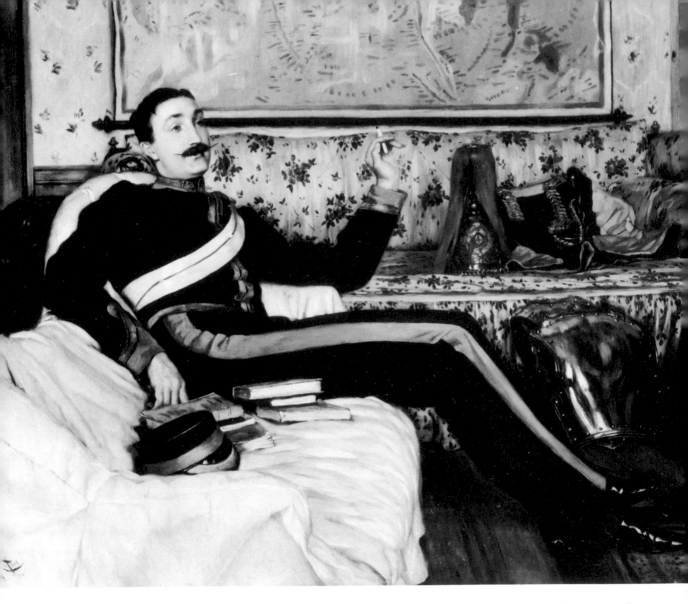

Colonel Fred Burnaby, Royal Horse Guards (The Blues), who joined the Relief Expedition in an unofficial capacity and was killed at Abu Klea. Celebrated as an athlete, marksman and horseman, and for a book about his travels in Central Asia *The Ride to Khiva*. Wounded at El Teb when attached to Graham's Intelligence Department. Painting dated 1870 by J.G. Tissot.

boxes. Picquets of the Mounted Infantry and the Naval Brigade with the Gardner were positioned on high ground to the left but the hills to the right, thought to be out of rifle range, were unoccupied. After dark groups of enemy snipers took up positions upon them.

There was little rest for the Desert Column that night. As always in the desert it was very cold, any light attracted a hail of bullets and, as Lieutenant Count Gleichen of the Grenadiers observed, 'On all sides arose the noise of tom-toms, now far away in the darkness and now so close that it seemed as if the whole of the enemy must be mustering for attack within three hundred yards; it was very jumpy listening to them.' When dawn broke on the 17th, the harassing fire thickened up as the men moved about to get warm and ate a quick breakfast of bully beef and biscuit. Casualties began to fall, including five officers wounded, and Stewart decided that, rather than await an attack, he would have to take the offensive if the wells were to be reached that day.

Leaving the wounded, the baggage and most of the camels in the zariba guarded by a party of Royal Sussex, he formed a square for the ad-

Officers of the Desert Column on the morning of Abu Klea. Centre mounted is Sir H. Stewart with Burnaby (dark jacket) at his horse's head. At left centre is Lord Charles Beresford RN pointing towards his sailors' Gardner gun which jammed at a critical moment. Print after Dickenson and Foster.

vance. Along the front face, from left to right, were half the Mounted Infantry, the screw-gun battery, the Coldstream and Scots Guards companies. Down the right face were the rest of the Guards, Grenadiers and Marines, and the balance of the Royal Sussex. On the rear face were four companies of the Heavies with the Naval Brigade and its Gardner gun in the centre, while the square was completed on the left by No. 5 Company of the Heavies and the other two companies of Mounted Infantry.[8] On each face the men were formed in double rank but the left face only mustered 235 rifles in contrast to 300 or more on each of the other three. In the centre were the staff and about 150 camels loaded with water, food, ammunition, hospital stores and cacolets[9] for the wounded. The Hussars and dismounted skirmishers of the Mounted Infantry and Scots Guards were pushed out to the flanks.

When all was ready the slow advance began, the movement immediately attracting a heavy fire which the skirmishers did their best to neutralise. The march followed the line of a valley down the centre of which ran a broad watercourse filled with clumps of long grass and scrub. To avoid this the square had to march across undulating ground on the right which slowed down the progress of the camels in the centre. Some way ahead to the left stretched a line of flags diagonally across the watercourse, thought by some to mark the enemy's main position, though others fancied an attack would come from the right where the enemy rifle-fire had been heaviest.

When within about 500 yards of these flags, the square was halted to allow the rear face, which had been delayed by the lagging camels, to close up. Before this could be completed a mass of some 5000 Arabs sprang up from the scrub and hurled themselves in two columns

[8] The Guards and Mounted Infantry Regiments each had four companies, the Heavies five. The MI were drawn from: KRRC (ninety men), Rifle Brigade and Royal West Kent (sixty each), South Staffords, Black Watch, Gordons, Royal Sussex, Essex, DCLI, Somerset LI, Connaught Rangers, Royal Scots Fusiliers (thirty each).

[9] Chairs made of iron and wood attached to pack-saddles.

The Battle of Abu Klea, 17 January 1885, at the moment the Mahdists broke into the left rear corner of the square against the Heavy Camel Regiment. Painting by W.B. Wollen.

Opposite: The Mounted Infantry detachment of the Queen's Own Royal West Kent Regiment with Lieutenant E.A. Alderson, commanding, in centre.

The square at Gubat or Abu Kru, 19 January 1885, where the Guards and Mounted Infantry Camel Regiments drove off the enemy blocking the way to the Nile. Print after Dickenson and Foster.

towards the left front corner of the square. The Mounted Infantry skirmishers immediately raced back to rejoin their regiment but their reitrement masked the fire which had to be withheld until the enemy were about 200 yards away. The 7-pounders came into action with shrapnel and the Mounted Infantry with rapid volleys. So effective was this fire that the enemy masses veered to their right where the ground was more broken, and joined up with three more columns to charge at great speed against the left rear corner of the square. Here acute danger threatened. A 60–80 yard gap had previously developed between the Heavies' No. 5 Company (5th and 16th Lancers) on the left face and No. 4 Company (Royal Dragoons and Scots

Greys) on the rear. Part of the latter company had been quickly moved to the left face but the opening remained. To fill it, Beresford had the Gardner gun manhandled twenty yards outside the left rear corner and opened fire on the onrushing enemy. At the same time Colonel Burnaby ordered No. 3 Company (4th and 5th Dragoon Guards) to wheel outwards from the rear face to support Beresford's gun on its left. The remaining two companies of the Heavies (Household Cavalry and 2nd Dragoon Guards) began edging to their right to support their comrades while the Sussex from the right face tried to thicken up the now attenuated rear.

At the very moment when the yelling Arabs were almost up to the square, the Gardner

jammed. It was instantly overrun, all the sailors being killed and Beresford himself only escaping by falling under the gun. Burnaby immediately ordered No. 3 Company to wheel back to its former position but, so furious was the Arabs' onset, that before the Dragoon Guards could reform the frenzied mass poured like a torrent into their original space as well as the gap behind the Gardner. The massive Burnaby fought single-handed with his sword for a few moments but, despite Corporal MacIntosh of the Blues dashing out to help his colonel, the odds were too great and both men fell under the spear-thrusts. The rear portion of the square was now a confused tumult of savage hand-to-hand fighting as the disordered Heavies and Sussex battled for their lives with their bayonets against the stabbing spears and slashing swords of the ever-increasing warriors. Had it not been for the solid clump of camels in the centre, the weight and impetus of the enemy charge must have carried it right across the square upon the rear of the hitherto unengaged front and right faces. Fortunately these were on slightly higher ground and, though shaken by the crowd of camels and Heavies pressed back against them, the rear ranks of the Guards and Mounted Infantry coolly faced about and opened a heavy, close-range musketry into the packed enemy spearmen, stolidly firing away with their Martinis as fast as they could work their extractor levers. Seeing their brothers now falling in heaps, the more rearward Arabs began to waver and fall back, away from the hail of heavy bullets smashing into their defenceless bodies which no amount of fanatical valour could protect. A band of enemy horsemen made a last attempt to retrieve the earlier success with a wild charge against the right rear corner but were driven off by the volleys of the Sussex and the Life Guards. By then the only Mahdists remaining inside the square were their dead and dying. The whole fierce action had lasted barely ten minutes.

Out of the enemy force estimated at between 8000 and 14000, 1100 bodies were counted in or near the square and many more had been wounded. During the day's fighting the Desert Column had lost nine officers and sixty-five men killed and another nine officers and eighty-five men wounded, two of the officers dying of their wounds. For a small force, isolated in a pitiless terrain and impelled by the need to drive on, these were serious losses, particularly for such a brief engagement. Chiefly affected were the Heavies who, though having fought gallantly, had demonstrated that soldiers trained throughout their service as cavalrymen could not, in their very first action against a ferocious and fast-moving enemy, be expected to produce the rock-like steadiness and disciplined musketry of trained infantry which alone could withstand the rapidity and fanaticism of charging warriors – as had been ably and timely delivered by the Foot Guards, Mounted Infantry and Sussex. Nevertheless this curiously constituted force – described sardonically by an officer of the River Column as 'London Society on camels' – had held its own against vastly superior numbers, and the way through to the by-now desperately needed water of Abu Klea wells was clear.

By the time the column had been rested, watered, fed and re-united with its baggage and camels it was not until 4 pm the next day that it was ready to move on. Metemmeh and the Nile were still twenty-three miles away and as time was of the essence the troops had to endure a most difficult and confused night march. It was 7.30 on the morning of the 19th before the weary men got their first distant glimpse of the river. It was, however, certain that it would not be reached without another fight, for large numbers of Arabs could be seen streaming out of Metemmeh, while others were already in position between the column and the river. The force halted, breakfasted and then began the construction of a zariba for the protection of the stores and animals, prior to advancing on foot in square as at Abu Klea. The work went ahead under an increasingly heavy rifle-fire from enemy marksmen creeping forward through the scrub. At 10 am Stewart received a serious wound in the groin which incapacitated him from further command. This was a severe blow, both for him and his men, for with the most suitable successor, Burnaby, now dead at Abu Klea, the command perforce devolved upon Sir Charles Wilson, a highly qualified intelligence officer but no fighting soldier. The harassing fire continued all morning, hampering the building of the defences, but by 2.30 in furtherance of Stewart's original plan the square was formed, ready to push on the last four miles to the river, while half the Heavies, the 19th Hussars, the artillery and the sailors guarded the zariba.

In the square the Marines and Grenadiers manned the front face, the Coldstream and Scots the right, the Heavies and Sussex the rear and the Mounted Infantry the left. As the march began the enemy rifle-fire intensified but, as Wilson wrote later, 'the men's faces were set in a determined way which meant business, and I knew they intended to drink from the Nile that night'. Along a ridge leading to the villages of Abu Kru and Gubat large numbers of enemy could be seen, their flags streaming out while the tom-toms throbbed continuously. The marching square received some fire support from the guns and the Gardner in the zariba and occasionally halted to fire its own volleys at the hidden riflemen. As the ridge was approached the enemy masses rose up, preparing to charge. The square halted, the men cheered and the volleys began crashing out from the double ranks as soon as the horde started flooding down the slopes. They came on at great speed, horsemen with banners in front, but when, as Gleichen described, 'they got

within 400 yards the volley-firing became a continuous roar of musketry, and hundreds fell beneath the well-directed fire of the Mounted Infantry and ourselves. Aiming low, firing steadily as on parade, our men mowed the Arabs down like grass; not one got within eighty yards of the square. At last the masses of the enemy in reserve, seeing the fate of the charging lines, wavered, scattered and bolted over the hills towards Metemmeh, and the river was won!'

The cool discipline and accurate fire of the infantrymen had prevented any recurrence of the close-quarter fighting of Abu Klea, but even so the day had cost the column another twenty-three killed and ninety-eight wounded, including three officers. Furthermore most of the men had been under fire, marching or working in exhausting conditions for three sweltering days and chilly nights with little rest, limited food and rather less water. The Nile had now been reached, and welcome its waters were to the tired and parched soldiers, but Metemmeh, two miles downstream from the point reached and the Desert Column's objective, was still in Mahdist hands. More alarming was the absence of any sign of Gordon's steamers, the vital link with Khartoum, still nearly a hundred miles away.

Nor did they come the following day, the whole of which was taken up with concentrating the whole force in a defensive position around Gubat, the precious hours slipping past while Wilson pondered what to do next. His deliberations resulted on the next day, the 21st, in a hesitant and, for the troops, frustrating attempt on Metemmeh, which Captain Marling[10] castigated in his diary, 'Nothing could have been more disgraceful than the dispositions made for the attack. We were actually marched up in square to within 800 yards of a loopholed town with guns, and kept paraded in front of it without advancing for over three hours, and when we retired we (presented) to the enemy the largest target possible.'

Wilson had been at a loss to know what to do,

---

[10] An experienced officer of the Mounted Infantry (60th Rifles) who had won the Victoria Cross at Tamai.

Preparing the village of Abu Kru for defence while the square under Sir Charles Wilson, on skyline to right, advanced against Metemmeh, 21 January. Eyewitness sketch by Melton Prior who accompanied the Desert Column.

Sir Charles Wilson embarking at Gubat with Captain Trafford's detachment of 1st Royal Sussex for the final dash to Khartoum on 24 January. Engraving after a sketch by Melton Prior.

but his dilemma had been diverted by the sudden and fortuitous appearance of the steamers from Khartoum. There were four, commanded by one of Gordon's ablest subordinates, Khasm-el-Mus, with some small brass guns and 200 enthusiastic soldiers, 'all fine men, mostly coal-black Negroes, attired in a fez, a shirt, a cartridge-belt and a rifle'. Khasm-el-Mus reported to Wilson that a large Mahdist force was on its way down-river and handed over Gordon's journal written up to 14 December with its prophetic words about Khartoum's possible fall around Christmas Day, and some of his private letters, one of which made the same forecast. However there was also a note in Gordon's hand, dated 29 December, which in contrast stated, 'Khartoum all right, could hold out for years.'

Now that the Desert Column had linked up with the steamers there was nothing to prevent Wilson from setting off to contact Gordon in compliance with Wolseley's orders; indeed Khasm-el-Mus was anxious to leave immediately. But Wilson formed the view that, in the light of reports of enemy forces advancing from north and south, he could not depart without first reconnoitring up and down the river to discover whether the column was in danger of attack. He later justified the delay this would entail by his opinion that, since Khartoum's fall had been deferred – due perhaps to the Desert Column's advance and losses inflicted on the enemy – 'there was nothing to show that the expected crisis would occur within the next few days.'

The whole of the 22nd was thus taken up with reconnaissances: by Wilson himself down-river to the north with three of the steamers, and by the 19th Hussars to the south. Neither revealed any imminent danger but much of the next day then had to be taken up with repairs and collection of fuel for the ships, as well as some re-arrangement of the crews. The original plan of manning them with the Naval Brigade had to be abandoned owing to its casualties suffered during the march, particularly among the officers and petty officers, all of whom had been killed or wounded, while Beresford himself was laid low in hospital with a painful boil on his bottom. At 3 pm the ships were reported ready but now Wilson could see no point in leaving before morning – despite four more days having been lost.

Accompanied by two of his staff, Captain Gascoigne and Lieutenant Stuart-Wortley, Wilson embarked with the 240 Sudanese soldiers and Captain Trafford with twenty men of the Royal Sussex aboard the steamers *Bordein* and *Telahawiyeh*. Mindful of the importance Gordon had attached to red coats being visible among the relief force, the Royal Sussex were tricked out in some outsize garments of that colour which the Guards had been carrying in their kits. At eight o'clock on the morning of 24 January the two little steamers pulled away, heading at last for Khartoum.

Within the besieged and wretched town conditions belied the optimistic note of nearly a month before. The lonely, tired but undaunted Gordon, his hair now white from strain, had continued to encourage his starving and lacklustre followers with assurances that help would soon come. On 20 January – three days after Abu Klea – the Mahdist guns had fired a victory salute, but Gordon learned from a spy that this was a ruse to conceal a defeat. Indeed in the enemy camp the news of Abu Klea had caused considerable vacillation among the Mahdi's emirs. As rumours of the British victory and the arrival at Metemmeh percolated into Khartoum, so the embattled garrison's spirits and resolve lifted, expecting every hour to see the returning steamers. When they did not come, despair set in and on the very day Wilson sailed Gordon's chief followers urged him to accept the Mahdi's terms for surrender. But however irresolute the Mahdist emirs and Khartoum notables were, nothing swayed the inflexible will of either the Mahdi or Gordon. On the 25th, determined to finish Khartoum before the relief column could arrive, the Mahdi ordered an attack for the following day. From the Palace roof, where for weeks he had searched the northern horizon for signs of rescue, Gordon watched the enemy preparations. He ordered that everyone, from eight years old to eighty, was to man the defences and hold them for twenty-four hours by which time the British

were sure to come. Having made what arrangements he could, he retired to his room and the only solace that remained to him: the smoking of endless cigarettes.

Throughout the 24th and 25th Wilson's progress was unimpeded, though occasional stops had to be made to collect more fuel which the steamers consumed in great quantity. Then, on the evening of the second day, the *Bordein* ran aground. Not without difficulty she was freed, only to do the same on the 26th. The delays thus caused lost almost twenty-four hours. They steamed on through the 27th until, at 11 am on the 28th, Khartoum was finally sighted in the distance. Soon the ships came under heavy fire from the banks, which grew in intensity as they approached the town. Still the steamers forged on, firing back with rifles and the brass guns,

The death of General Gordon at Khartoum on 26 January, as reconstructed in the painting by George Joy. Some accounts claim that Gordon was in a white uniform.

while Wilson and his officers anxiously searched through their binoculars for a sight of the Egyptian flag flying from the town. But there was no flag, neither in the town nor from the roof of Gordon's Palace where it had always flown. Notwithstanding the bombardment, they drew closer still, but the chanting crowds and flaunting banners along the bank, the shells coming from Khartoum itself, the wrecked Palace, all told a tale that could no longer be denied. They were too late; Khartoum had fallen. With heavy heart the despondent Wilson ordered the ships to turn and sail back the way they had come.

Two days before, in the early hours of the 26th, the Mahdists had swarmed into the town, overrunning the disheartened and weakened defenders. Within an hour all resistance ceased and the Arabs embarked on an orgy of slaughter and pillage. Accounts of how Gordon met his end vary, but none deny that he confronted his enemies with the high courage he had always shown. Whether he was speared unresisting on the Palace steps or shot fighting to the last will never be known for sure, but they cut off his head and bore it in triumph to the Mahdi who had expressly ordered that Gordon's life should be spared. When the dreadful trophy was brought to him, he was enraged.

Serving with the Desert Column as an intelligence officer was Major Kitchener of the Royal Engineers, last met as a subaltern spying out the defences of Alexandria in 1882. In August 1885 he submitted a report on the fall of Khartoum which concluded with these words: 'The memorable siege of Khartoum lasted 317 days, and it is not too much to say that such a noble resistance was due to the indomitable resolution and resource of one Englishman. Never was a garrison so nearly rescued, never was a commander so sincerely lamented'. In the fullness of time it would fall to Kitchener to avenge that resolute Englishman, a fellow-Sapper and his own inspiration.

111

9

A Spirited Policy

Wilson and his disconsolate little band eventually reached the Desert Column safely on 4 February. He had lost both ships, wrecked, and had had to be rescued by a now recovered Beresford, who had made an epic voyage in the *Safieh*, surviving the dangers of Mahdist shore batteries and a burst boiler. The sad news of Khartoum had already reached Gubat on the 1st, brought by Stuart-Wortley in a rowing boat. For the men of the Camel Corps, who had striven so hard, and had daily waited anxiously as much for fresh supplies as for news, the feeling, as expressed by Gleichen, was that 'all our fighting and the lives of so many of our men

had been thrown away for nothing; as usual the Government had sent us too late.' At Korti, where Wolseley, forbidden by the Government to accompany either column, had been eating his heart out with frustration, the news came in on the evening of the 4th. He vented his fury and disappointment in his journal, laying the blame wholly on the Prime Minister. 'If anything can kill old Gladstone this news ought to, for he cannot, self-illusionist though he be,

Lord Charles Beresford aboard *Safieh* engaging the Mahdist shore batteries during his voyage to rescue Sir Charles Wilson. Beresford is to the left of the three sailors manning the gun. Engraving by W.H. Overend.

disguise from himself that he is directly responsible'.

In England, when the Queen was informed by telegraph on the 5th, she fired off a salvo at Gladstone, Granville and Hartington, berating them for not having acted sooner. The nation, whose hopes had been raised by the successes of the Camel Corps, was gripped by shock and anger. In the music halls they sang, 'Too late, too late to save him/In vain, in vain they tried/His life was England's glory/His death was England's pride.' A leader in the *Graphic* suggested that the public's 'grief for the death of the defender of Khartoum will be mingled with execration for the Ministers who sacrificed him through their incurable vacillation'. Gladstone, the Grand Old Man, became for many the Murderer Of Gordon. Many thought the Government must fall but Gladstone just survived, largely through a Cabinet decision, after some prodding by the Queen, that Wolseley should be given a free hand in the Sudan to crush the Mahdi, and that a second expedition should be sent to Suakin to destroy Osman Digna, prior to constructing a railway onwards to Berber.

After Gordon's death, Wolseley had been unable to decide how to proceed. The fall of Khartoum had deprived his expedition not only of its mission – the relief of Gordon – but had released all the Mahdist forces for further action against his two separated columns which could now be overwhelmed by the enemy's enormous numerical superiority. When he first learned of the Government's new intentions on 6 February he was astounded, confiding to his journal that they must have been inspired for 'party purposes to keep Mr Gladstone in office' and by the Cabinet's realisation that 'nothing could save them except a spirited policy'. It seemed to him that such a policy could not be implemented before the autumn, because the destruction of the Mahdi had not been contemplated when the size and composition of the original relief expedition had been settled, and would require considerable reinforcements which would take months to arrive. In the meantime, however, there would be advantage in seizing Berber; this could have a moral effect over the

Major-General W. Earle, commanding the River Column. He fought as a junior regimental officer in the major battles of the Crimean War, was promoted major-general in 1880, and commanded the base and lines of communication in the Egyptian War. Killed at Kirbekan.

wavering tribes who had not yet thrown in their lot with the Mahdi, it would provide a base for an eventual offensive, and would also assist the new force operating out of Suakin. He therefore planned to use both the River and Desert Columns to this end.

After first hearing of Stewart's serious wound at Gubat, Wolseley had despatched Buller with the 1st Royal Irish to take over the Desert Column, but on learning of Gordon's death, had ordered him to prepare to withdraw with the Column to Jakdul Wells. On receipt of the Government's new instructions, he sent Buller fresh orders on 10 February, telling him to take Metemmeh prior to co-operating with Earle and the River Column in the capture of Berber. By the time these orders reached Buller, it was, as will be seen, too late. The River Column which – due to great difficulties over

Battle of Kirbekan, 10 February 1885. Attacking the enemy right from the rear are the 1st Black Watch, while the 1st South Staffords skirmish towards the river. Other South Staffords' companies are attacking the enemy centre in the far distance at left. The stone hut is where General Earle was killed. An engraving – after a sketch by a South Staffords' officer – by R. Caton Woodville, who has shown the Highlanders' helmet hackles on the wrong side.

the boats, the cataracts and supply problems – had only managed to traverse sixty miles by the time it heard of Khartoum's fall, had been halted on the 5th. Three days later it was ordered to advance again to Abu Hamed for Wolseley's proposed joint attack on Berber.

Earle was not one of Wolseley's Ring and Wolseley, though liking him as a man, originally had doubts about his capacity for command at the start of the campaign but later came to value his qualities. Ian Hamilton of the

Gordons, who saw much of Earle on the Nile, described him as 'that old martinet', but also considered him 'a bold man who had kept himself in touch with the rank and file and was out for fighting'. To compensate for Earle's lack of organisational ability, Wolseley gave him, as principal staff officer and second-in-command, Colonel Henry Brackenbury, very much of the Ring, and in Hamilton's view a 'bureaucratic, scholastic soldier' who 'in sheer brain power was chronologically one thousand years in advance of (Earle)'. Under this combination of widely disparate talents the River Column resumed its advance.

On the next day the squadron of 19th Hussars scouting along the left bank encountered an Arab force holding a line of hillocks at right angles to the river, behind which and parallel to it, was a higher ridge, the Jebel

Kirbekan, also held in strength. Earle's four battalions were strung out along the river but he had readily to hand, besides the Hussars, the 1st South Staffords and 1st Black Watch as well as a troop of Egyptian Army Camel Corps with two guns. He decided to attack without waiting for his other battalions to come up. Colonel Butler, who had been commanding the advance guard, had discovered a deep, wide wadi which would permit a covered approach right round the eastern end of the Jebel. Earle, who at first had been bent on a frontal attack, was persuaded to use this so as to outflank the enemy positions and attack them from the rear, thus cutting off their line of retreat.

Having disembarked and left the baggage and boats guarded by a Black Watch company, the two guns and two companies of the Staffords went forward to engage the enemy on the hillocks from the front. Then, at 7.15 am, covered by the Hussars ahead and the Egyptian camelry on the left, the infantry began its flank march, led by Colonel Eyre's South Staffords. After an hour and a quarter the force came in line with the eastern end of the Jebel at which moment the Egyptian guns and Camel Corps opened fire from the front to engage the enemy's attention. As the column wheeled left to advance along the rear of the position, it was observed and fired on from the Jebel. Eyre led up two of his companies, supported by fire from a third, to attack the western end, but so accurate was the enemy fire that the companies became pinned down in the rocks and Eyre was killed.

Meanwhile the Black Watch pushed on towards the river bank, turned left and attacked the hillocks from the rear with the three remaining Staffords companies in support. As they were about to launch their final charge, a body of Arab spearmen made a headlong counterattack upon the nearest Black Watch company. The Highlanders stood firm and this brave attempt withered away under the steady volleys. The charge then went in, with pipers playing, until the enemy were driven from their rocky positions. At that moment of victory, as the troops were clearing the area, General Earle was suddenly killed by a shot from a hut where some enemy had hidden. Brackenbury immediately assumed command. Hearing that Eyre's assault on the Jebel had failed and the enemy there still held out, he at once ordered the uncommitted Staffords to the attack. Not to be outdone by the Highlanders, this they did with great dash. Advancing up the slopes in short rushes, they took the summit with the bayonet, killing every man of the enemy who stood to the last.

It was now 12.30. Some of the Arabs had managed to make their getaway across the Nile before the attack went in, but for the most part Earle's daring encirclement, his plain infantry tactics – 'open attack formations, none of your Abu Klea squares', as Hamilton wrote – had surprised and overwhelmed the enemy with complete success and slight loss: forty-seven wounded and ten killed, three of them officers. It was a tragedy, and a commentary on this type of warfare, that one was the General himself, another a battalion commander. That evening Earle's body, together with those of Eyre and Coveney of the Black Watch, were buried by both regiments beside a lone tree on the bank of the Nile, where 'the rugged rock desert of the Monassir spreads its awful desolation.'[11]

Brackenbury was undoubtedly very clever, an excellent planner and far ahead of his time, but he had the reputation of being more at home in an office than in the field. He was by temperament a staff officer rather than a commander. Nevertheless he had successfully completed what Earle had begun, and he now applied his quick brain to the problem of getting the River Column through the difficult country and dangerous rapids that lay ahead; he soon appreciated that all would take much longer than the optimistic Earle had estimated. At the end of a fortnight they had only managed about four miles a day and Abu Hamed was still another 30 miles on and Berber 150 miles. However the way ahead was now easier and Brackenbury hoped to speed up. The leading boats were just about to move off on 24 February when a messenger arrived from Wolseley. The column was to turn about and return immediately. The

[11] Colonel W.F. Butler, *The Campaign of the Cataracts*.

Standard or *raya* of a Mahdist emir. Each was supposed to bear the legend, 'Mohammed el Mahdi is the Khalifa of the Prophet of God', to which extracts from the Koran were added.

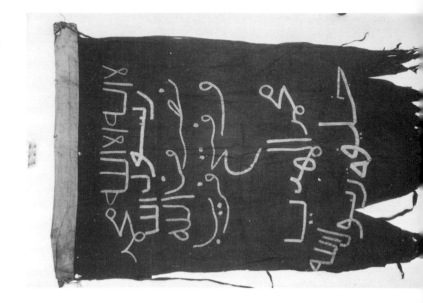

2nd Life Guards detachment of the Heavy Camel Regiment after its return to England. Trousers have replaced breeches and puttees which became totally worn out during the campaign.

whole long haul up-river – three and a half months and nearly 550 miles at the oars of the whalers – had been for nothing. The only consolation for the infantry oarsmen who had worked so hard and so uncomplainingly was, as Hamilton put it: 'We flew back on the plumeless, foam-flecked wings of the cataract which had so furiously fought against our advance.'

What had upset Wolseley's plans was Buller's discovery, on reaching Gubat on 11 February, that such was the broken-down state of the Desert Column's camels that further operations from Gubat were out of the question. On his own initiative, before Wolseley's orders about taking Berber had even reached him, he ordered a retreat to Abu Klea. Heartened by Buller's great red face and unruffled demeanour, the Camel Corps trudged back the way they had come but now on foot, most of the remaining camels being needed for the sick and wounded. A large force of Arabs shadowed the weary march but, with the Royal Irish steady as rearguard, the wells were reached safely, though the camp was subjected to continuous harassing musketry during the six days spent there. At length, conscious of the inadequate forage and water, not to mention the threat of superior numbers, Buller retreated again to Jakdul. It was here that Herbert Stewart finally succumbed to the wound he had received a month before and borne under such painful conditions. Before he died, he wrote Wolseley a moving letter, thanking him for his many kindnesses and hoping he would speak well of his efforts to Lady Stewart.

When news of Buller's retirement first reached Wolseley, he had planned to divert the Desert Column to Merowi, thirty miles northeast of Korti, there to support the River Column. But by 18 February he had fully grasped that the Desert Column was unfit for further operations, not only because of the hopeless state of its transport but also because the men's boots were thoroughly worn out. This fact, together with a report from Brackenbury that the River Column was unlikely to reach Berber before 12 March, thus eating up more supplies than had been allowed for, convinced Wolseley that all operations would have to be postponed until the autumn. Orders went out on 20 February for all troops to return to Korti, prior to moving into summer quarters along the Nile between Merowi and the 3rd Cataract below Dongola. The River Column returned on 7 March and nine days later the rearguard of the Desert Column marched in.

After all the hardships, sacrifices and disappointments it looked as though the best Wolseley's men could expect was an uncomfortable, possibly dangerous and very hot summer under canvas. One officer, the 'useless' Colonel Stanley Clarke, wasted little time in forming up to Wolseley to plead the Prince of Wales's need for him at home. Wolseley was thankful to see the back of him, taking the opportunity to tell him 'he did not come up to the mark'. A few others went with him for various reasons but most prepared to make the best of things. As will be seen, events far from the Nile would affect the pursuit of the 'spirited policy', but for the moment the focus moves east to Suakin where, on the very day the Nile force was moving into its new camps, the other expedition was going into action.

10

Last Stand At Suakin

After Graham's operations around Suakin the year before, Osman Digna had lain comparatively low, confining his hostility to pin-prick attacks against the small garrison Graham had left behind. During the Nile campaign the question of some action to occupy Osman Digna's attention had been considered between the Government in London, Baring in Cairo and Wolseley in the desert but, largely in deference to the latter's viewpoint, nothing was done except to reinforce the Suakin garrison with a battalion in mid-January. After Khartoum's fall Wolseley had recommended a force be sent to crush Osman Digna, to which the Government acceded when it determined to continue operations against the Mahdi. The command was again given to Graham who was instructed, first to defeat Osman Digna in the field; second to occupy the territory adjoining the Suakin-Berber route, with a view to protecting the construction of the railway (for which a contract was given to a civilian firm); and third to link up with the Nile Army which by then should have occupied Berber. Thus, when the autumn campaign against the Mahdi began, both routes to Khartoum, up the Nile and from the Red Sea coast, would be in British hands. When in February it became clear that Berber could not, after all, be taken in the spring, Graham was told to halt when he reached Ariab, 150 miles from Berber.

The force he was allotted was more than twice the size of that he had commanded the year before – some 13,000 fighting men – and was of interesting composition. A Guards Brigade was sent out from England, while a second infantry brigade was formed of troops already in the theatre of operations.[12] A cavalry brigade of the 5th Lancers and 20th Hussars was completed by a battalion of Mounted Infantry. Artillery support was provided by three batteries, one Royal Horse Artillery, one mountain and one field. Three companies of Royal Engineers were accompanied by two telegraph sections and a novelty in the shape of a balloon detachment. In addition a brigade was sent from India, including the 9th Bengal Cavalry, three battalions and a company of Madras Sappers. The Indian Government also supplied a large quantity of animal transport and over 4000 camel drivers, muleteers, bhisties, dhooly bearers and labourers.[13]

The last contingent to join gave the expedition a truly Imperial flavour. As a gesture of solidarity in the wake of Gordon's death, the Government of New South Wales offered and despatched an infantry battalion and an artillery battery. The men of the infantry were not regular soldiers like the British and Indian troops but volunteers who enlisted specially for the campaign. Many of them were British born and with previous military experience – for example, the Regimental-Sergeant-Major, Michael Tuite, had served in the Maori Wars of the 1860s and in Afghanistan – but even so the battalion represented a cross-section of New South Wales society. One soldier, Robert Hunter, recalled serving with 'men of all classes, some of whom had left good homes, comfort and good positions', which was echoed by Private Dick who recorded that 'high government officials, bankers, clerks, old soldiers, businessmen of every grade fought for a position in the ranks.' This campaign was to be the debut of Australian soldiers in war and the first occasion when white troops of the Empire went to the aid of the Mother Country overseas.

---

[12] *Guards Brigade*: 3rd Grenadiers, 1st Coldstream, 2nd Scots Guards. *Infantry Brigade*: 2nd East Surrey, 1st Berkshire, 1st Shropshire Light Infantry, Royal Marine Light Infantry.

[13] bhisties are water carriers; a dhooly is a litter for wounded.

Lieutenant-General Sir Gerald Graham VC (fourth from left) with members of his staff at Suakin. Fifth from right is an Italian liaison officer from Massawa.

By mid-March the whole force, less the Australians who did not arrive until the 29th, was concentrated around Suakin. The great assemblage of troops and mass of shipping offshore had not escaped Osman Digna, who promptly sent in a defiant letter to Graham. In reply the latter warned the Hadendoa that unless he submitted he would be crushed, reminding him of his defeats at El Teb and Tamai. Needless to say, no submission was forthcoming. The main enemy force of some 7000 was thought to be around Tamai, but another body of about 1200 was at Hashin, from where night raids on Suakin had been made and which could threaten the right flank of any advance against Tamai to the south. Graham therefore decided to deal first with Hashin and establish an outpost there.

On 20 March he advanced with his three infantry brigades and the cavalry. The terrain around Hashin was dominated by a number of steep, rocky hills rising abruptly from the plain which was scoured by dried-up watercourses and covered in dense, prickly mimosa bushes from six to eight feet high. The latter provided excellent cover for the Hadendoa riflemen and spearmen and made the going difficult for formed bodies of troops. The 2nd East Surrey with British and Indian sappers seized a three-peaked hill to the right of the line of advance and began to construct redoubts upon it. With their flanks protected by cavalry, the 1st Berkshire and Marines attacked a steep ridge under rifle fire, while on their right the Indian Brigade went forward supported by the Guards. As the enemy were driven from the ridge on to the low ground below, they were pursued by two squadrons of the 9th Bengal Cavalry. However the pursuit was carelessly handled and one squadron, dismounted to fire volleys, was surprised by Arab spearmen springing out of the undergrowth and had to ride back hurriedly to the protection of the Guards' square. On the right the Indian infantry had some skirmishing

Above: Officers of 3rd Battalion Grenadier Guards at Windsor Castle on 19 February 1885 before leaving for the Sudan. Sixth from left is Colonel Hon. W. Home, the commanding officer.

Below: Officers of the same battalion a few weeks later at Suakin. Most have now grown beards.

Below: Private Tom Gunning of the New South Wales Infantry in the service dress sent from England for issue to the Australians on arrival at Suakin.

against some scattered enemy and the 5th Lancers made a successful charge, but around midday they were ordered to retire, covered by the brigade on the ridge, which then retired in turn. Both brigades went back in squares to below the East Surreys' position, their movement covered by the RHA guns and the Guards who fell back, also in square, firing volleys at the enemy who re-occupied the ridge and kept up a hot fire from the scrub. At 2.30 pm, leaving the East Surreys in their redoubt, the whole force marched back to Suakin. In his despatch afterwards Graham admitted that the action had not been decisive since it had not been possible to inflict the heavy casualties the enemy must have suffered had they charged his squares as he had hoped. On the other hand, the installation of the East Surreys' redoubts prevented the nightly attacks on Suakin, and had secured the right flank of the projected advance against Tamai.

To effect this, Graham intended to establish an intermediate outpost to contain and protect the ammunition, water and supplies needed when out of range of Suakin. On 22 March Major-General McNeill marched out with a convoy of some 1500 transport animals and a strong escort of the 1st Berkshire, Royal Marines, the three Indian battalions, two sapper companies and a Naval detachment with four Gardner guns; the column was preceded by a squadron of the 5th Lancers. The infantry

marched in two squares, the Indian square enclosing all the transport, but such was the difficulty in maintaining this formation in the thick scrub that progress was slow and the camel convoy became increasingly disordered. McNeill therefore decided to set up the post at Tofrek, two miles short of the intended destination, so as to allow time for the work to be completed and for the Indian Brigade to return to Suakin before nightfall.

After halting at 10.30, work began on three zaribas: one central one for the stores and two smaller ones at the north-east and south-west corners, for the Marines and Berkshires respectively, each with two Gardners. Part of the force was cutting and dragging in the thorn scrub for the zaribas while others were kept under arms in covering parties. The approaches from the west, north of the Berkshire zariba, were watched by the 15th Sikhs; from the north, between the Sikhs and Marines, by the 28th Bombay Infantry and two companies of the 17th Bengal Infantry; while facing south were the rest of the 17th. The east, apart from the Marine zariba, was open, but half the Berkshires were some 250 yards east of the central zariba, partly as a reserve and partly to prevent the unloaded baggage animals and their drivers from straying back towards Suakin from where they were parked clear of the working parties. The 5th Lancers squadron formed 'cossack posts', each of four men, about a mile and a half out, but they could neither see nor be seen from the zaribas, so thick and high was the scrub. Indeed, with a perimeter of three miles to cover and the squadron under strength, the posts may have been as much as a quarter of a mile apart. Nothing had been seen of the enemy and the work went ahead undisturbed.

It was hot and tiring under the blazing sun and at 2.30 the Berkshire half-battalion east of the zariba piled arms to have a late meal. Suddenly a lancer rode in to report the enemy advancing in strength. McNeill at once had the alarm sounded. As the working parties ran to their arms, all the lancers came galloping back with many small darting groups of spearmen racing at their heels, almost alongside them, from all sides except the north. The 17th Bengal, their ranks disordered by the retreating cavalry, fired one volley and took to their heels. Parties of Arabs ran amongst the baggage animals, stampeding them and driving them towards the zaribas and the unprotected Berkshires in reserve. As soon as the latter had heard the alarm, they had dropped their mess-tins, seized their rifles and flung themselves into a firing line where they stood firm, killing some 200 with their volleys. The other half of their battalion scrambled into their zariba, only to find the Hadendoa swarming over the uncompleted barricade, rushing hither and

thither, cutting down the Gardner crews who had been unable to get their guns into action in time. Rapidly forming a square in one corner of the zariba the Berkshires grimly stuck it out and gradually their rapid firing got the upper hand. To the north the Sikhs threw back every rush made at them, maintaining their line intact and giving valuable support to the hard-pressed Berkshires. On the north side the 28th Bombay and the Marines were less directly engaged except on the east-facing side of the latter's zariba, which fortunately had been completed and thus broke the impetus of the enemy on-slaught. Everywhere the Arabs fought with fanatical courage and dash, but once the infantry had recovered from the suddenness of the charge, discipline and the Martini-Henry saved the day; the 'coffin-'eaded shield an' shovel-spear' of Kipling's Fuzzy-Wuzzy could not prevail against the .45 bullet. Nevertheless the force had undoubtedly been surprised, and if the two halves of the Berkshires, on whom the brunt fell, had not stood their ground, the speed and numbers of the 'big, black, boundin'' Hadendoa might well have 'crumpled up the square'. As it was the action had cost the lives of 117 officers and men, with a further 179 wounded or missing, together with 176 casualties among the followers and the loss of 501 camels. For the gallant and timely conduct of its 1st Battalion at Tofrek, the Queen later conferred upon the Berkshire Regiment the prefix 'Royal', only the second occasion when such an honour has been awarded for a single action.

In the following week more water and supplies were moved up to Tofrek, escorted by the Guards battalions. As the position was strengthened, the East Surreys were withdrawn from Hashin into reserve. The garrison of Tofrek was raised to four battalions, the Guards and Marines being rotated in turn, the Berkshires electing to remain on duty at the place they had made their own. A few attacks were launched at the convoys, but when Graham advanced against Tamai on 3 April with two brigades, which now included the Australians, there was little resistance and the enemy melted away into the hills to the south-west. In fact, after Tofrek, the Hadendoa never

THEATRE OF OPERATIONS AROUND SUAKIN, 1884–85

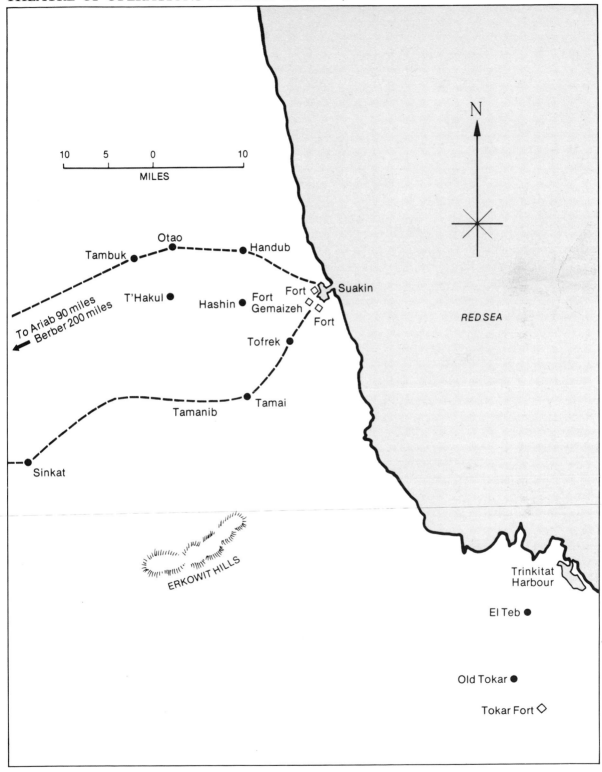

N

10   5   0   10
MILES

Tambuk ●   Otao ●   ● Handub

To Ariab 90 miles
Berber 200 miles

T'Hakul ●   Hashin ●   Fort
Gemaizeh
Fort ◇   ◇ Suakin
◇ Fort

Tofrek ●

RED SEA

Tamanib   Tamai ●

Sinkat ●

ERKOWIT HILLS

Trinkitat
Harbour

El Teb ●

Old Tokar ●

Tokar Fort ◇

Above: NCOs and sepoys of the 28th Bombay Infantry at Suakin. The Indian infantry were still armed with the Snider rifle, the predecessor of the British troops' Martini-Henry.

Opposite above: The hospital ship *Ganges* off-shore at Suakin. Three such ships supported the field force, including one specifically for the Indian troops.

Opposite: The action at Hashin, 20 March 1885, showing the 9th Bengal Cavalry sheltering in the Guards' square, The Indian Brigade is to the right rear in the gorge. Behind are the heights attacked by the 1st Berkshire Regiment and Royal Marines. Painting by T.S. Seccombe.

came on again in strength and in the remaining seven weeks of the campaign, the field force only lost one man killed and twenty-six wounded in action.

The growing heat and difficulties of water supply dissuaded Graham from pursuing Osman Digna into the hills. Tamai and large quantities of ammunition were destroyed and Graham turned his attention to opening up the route for the Berber railway. Friendly overtures were made to those local tribes disenchanted with Osman Digna, but with only limited success owing to Graham's inability to give them assurances of continued British protection. The railway line crept out into the desert, guarded at intervals by fortified posts and by strong patrols searching the neighbouring valleys for hostile Arabs. A camel corps was formed for this purpose from the British, Australian and Indian battalions. By the end of April the railway had reached Otao, twenty miles from Suakin. Learning of a hostile band assembling to harass the work from T'Hakul, south of Otao, Graham despatched a mobile force of the 9th Cavalry, Mounted Infantry and Camel Corps from

125

Opposite: The Battle of Tofrek, or McNeill's Zariba, 22 March 1885. The enemy, having broken through the 17th Bengal Infantry, stampede the camp followers and baggage camels towards the 1st Berkshire Regiment. Painting by C.E. Fripp, war artist of *The Graphic*.

Opposite below: British and Indian officers of the 15th Bengal Infantry (Ludhiana Sikhs) which, though heavily attacked, held firm on the west face of the zariba at Tofrek, thus protecting the rear of the Berkshires. Subadar Goordit Singh saved the lives of two Berkshire soldiers by placing himself between them and their attackers, killing three of the enemy with his sword.

Below: Royal Marines mopping up after the battle. Over a thousand enemy dead were counted around the zariba. Watercolour by C.E. Fripp.

Suakin to attack from the south, while the 15th Sikhs and more Mounted Infantry from Otao went in from the north. This well-planned little operation was entirely successful, not only in dispersing the enemy but in persuading the wavering tribes, even some of the Hadendoa, that their best interests lay with the British. Then suddenly all Graham's steady progress became pointless. Five days after the T'Hakul operation he learned from Wolseley that the Government had decided on complete evacuation of the whole Sudan by British forces.

This reversal of policy owed its origins to a skirmish thousands of miles away around a small caravanserai in Central Asia called Pandjeh, which lay just within the domains of the Amir of Afghanistan to whom Britain was bound by treaty. On 30 March a Russian general attacked and occupied it, thereby flouting the work of an Anglo-Russian Commission which at the time was attempting to settle the boundary between the Tsar's Asiatic provinces and Afghanistan. Once again Russian expansionism in Asia gave rise to fears for India's safety.

For Gladstone this was a Godsent oppor-

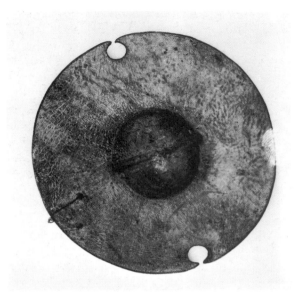

Left: Shield of hippopotamus hide used by the Hadendoa and taken at Tofrek.

Opposite: The railway constructed from Suakin towards Berber with a redoubt and watchtower beyond. The trucks bear the name, 'Lucas & Aird', the civilian contractors for the line.

Opposite below: Two of the casualties of the Sudan campaign 1884–85. *Left*: Private Steele, 4th Dragoon Guards attached Heavy Camel Regiment, wounded at Abu Klea by a deep sword cut across the back of the neck and another cut on the right temple. His neck remained permanently stiff. *Right*: Private Ryder, 1st Berkshire Regiment, wounded at Tofrek by a sword cut through left cheek, upper jaw and lip to lower lip, a spear wound in the left shoulder and a sword cut on the left wrist. His left hand was permanently disabled.

Below: Men of the New South Wales Contingent manning a redoubt, with a field gun and heliograph (right).

tunity to renege on the 'spirited policy' towards the Sudan. How could operations against the Mahdi be justified, politically and morally (the latter played fortissimo as always in Gladstonian rhetoric), when there loomed the possibility of war with Russia? At the time he carried his colleagues with him, obtaining a war credit of £11 million, and a telegram went in mid-April to Wolseley informing him that 'Imperial interests might necessitate withdrawal of all troops from Sudan and the concentration in Egypt of all those now up the Nile'. As usual Wolseley poured out his despairing rage into his journal against 'the old imposter Gladstone ... only too anxious to avail himself of the excuse of a threatened war with Russia, which he never means to embark in ... if he can possibly avoid it', and hoping that 'he be torn limb from limb by the people he has deceived'.

Wolseley naturally protested vehemently

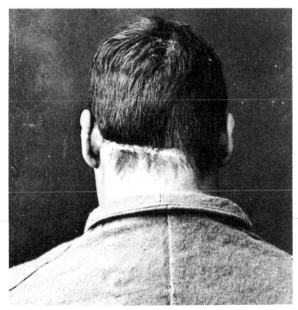

but ineffectually against abandoning the Sudan; the Afghan boundary question was settled by arbitration; and Gladstone, though he did not suffer the literal fate Wolseley wished for him, lost office in early June. By then, however, it was too late to reverse the evacuation process and the new Conservative Government accepted it. Throughout the summer of 1885 the troops of the Nile Expedition went back down the great river they had so laboriously and

hopefully ascended; some, like the Camel Corps, to return home, others into garrison in Egypt. From Suakin the Guards returned, welcomed by cheering crowds as they marched through London one evening in their tropical helmets and khaki drill fighting dress, while across the world, in similar kit, the New South Wales Contingent were 'enthusiastically fêted' in Sydney, despite the teeming rain.

In his final despatch on the whole campaign,

129

The last action of 1885, the battle of Ginniss, 30 December. Lieutenant-General Sir F. Stephenson (black horse) watching the 1st Yorkshire (Green Howards) advancing on the village supported by the guns of 2/1 Battery, South Irish Division, Royal Artillery. The Camerons attacked to the right of the guns and the other three battalions out of the picture to the left. Drawing by A. Forestier.

the last he would ever compile as a field commander, Wolseley wrote: 'The spirit and behaviour of the troops, whether on the Nile or at Suakin, may be viewed with satisfaction by every Englishman. No one can regret more than I do the fall [of Khartoum] but in common with all my countrymen, I look back with pride to the gallant struggle made by our troops to save Khartoum and its heroic defender.' A well-deserved tribute to the men who had done the work, but for Wolseley himself there were no accolades. On 13 July, suffering from acute diarrhoea, the bitterly disappointed general, whose career had once promised so much, reached London where 'the horrid fashionable crowd came to meet me at the station.' From that day, though only just fifty-two, he declined in health, in mental capacity and in professional competence. Though he was eventually to succeed Cambridge as Commander-in-Chief in 1895, he was by then a shadow of his former self and the office itself had already

succumbed to the reforms he had so often urged in the past. In a way Khartoum finished Wolseley as surely as it had finished Gordon.

Nor did his failure benefit the man he had struggled against. As the Dervish hordes spread northwards in the wake of the retreating British, the Mahdi was taken ill and on 20 June he died. The vacant leadership was immediately seized by the Khalifa Abdullah el-Taaishi who announced that, since the last thoughts of the Mahdi had been directed towards the conquest of Egypt, his wishes must be carried on.

By mid-December the Khalifa's invasion army was in touch with the outposts of the Anglo-Egyptian force established to guard the frontier around Wadi Halfa after the withdrawal of the Nile Expedition. The most advanced post, at Kosheh, was held by the Cameron Highlanders and two companies of the 9th Egyptians (Sudanese), who held out while reinforcements arrived from Cairo with General Stephenson in command. By 29 December he disposed of a force which, besides the Camerons, included the 20th Hussars, four British battalions[14] and elements of the Egyptian Army. On the penultimate day of 1885 Stephenson launched a dawn attack on the Dervishes at Ginniss on the banks of the Nile. By ten o'clock the enemy was a disorganised mass of fugitives, the Khalifa's first attempt on Egypt had failed, and the First Sudan War came to an end.

To these battalions had fallen the opportunity of extracting some revenge for the unhappy events of 1885. In doing so, they had also been the last to wear the British infantryman's scarlet in action, Stephenson sharing Gordon's view of the morale effect of that colour upon a savage enemy. Years were to pass before the Khalifa's mighty host again encountered the British Infantry and its devastating musketry, and by then its imposing scarlet tunic had been relegated to the parade ground.

[14] 1st Royal Berkshire, 1st Royal West Kent, 1st Yorkshire (Green Howards), 2nd Durham Light Infantry.

= PART III =

THE SUDAN
RECLAIMED

11

Holding the Frontier

By the end of 1885 Mahdism held the whole of the Sudan in its sway. Except for an Egyptian garrison at Suakin and a few small posts still maintained by Emin Pasha in Equatoria [15], the Khalifa's military power had replaced the hated 'Turk' in the land, even as far as the Egyptian frontier, halted there by the victory of Ginniss. Yet although the Egyptian overlords had been driven from the Sudan, the Khalifa had still to consolidate the position he had assumed and not all were unanimous in giving him their support. In the years following the Mahdi's death there would be plots, mutinies, insurrections and defections within the Sudan as well as hostility from without, from Abyssinia, from the Italians in their new colony of Eritrea on the Red Sea coast, and above all from Suakin and the Egyptian frontier. To the fears engendered by living in such cruel and uncertain times would in due course be added the miseries of plague and famine. There was thus much danger and misery for the peoples of the Sudan but, despite the turbulence and vastness of his domains, the Khalifa remained supreme, maintaining a balance of power among the various tribes, crushing any who overreached themselves, imprisoning or executing possible rivals. Gordon's head had been the first of many to be displayed in the Khalifa's new and ramshackle capital of Omdurman: rival emirs, failed or doubtful subordinates, even King John's of Abyssinia after a great struggle in 1889.

The Khalifa's power rested on armed might, his *Ansar*[16], the backbone of which were the *Mulazamin*, drawn from the sons of noted tribal leaders, and the black riflemen, the Bazingers or *Jehadia* formerly employed by the Egyptians. Initially, these had been formed as the Khalifa's bodyguard but they were to swell into a much larger force by the late 1890s. The Mulazamin and the Omdurman garrison, known as the Kara Army and also originating from the Jehadia, received regular pay, rations and training and were mostly armed with rifles, in contrast to the spears and swords of the tribal masses that made up the rest of the Ansar. But once the Mulazamin had outgrown the functions of a bodyguard, the Khalifa needed another body to oversee his army. This he found in his own tribe, the Taaisha, a section of the Baggara, whom he installed in Omdurman as a privileged and pampered elite before whom all quailed. With these instruments the Khalifa Abdullah – vain, ruthless, cunning and determined – subdued all who thwarted his will or threatened his power for thirteen years.

The defeat at Ginniss had set back the fulfilment of the Mahdi's dreams of the conquest of Egypt, and the bloody conflict with Abyssinia, which began in 1885, gave Egypt a breathing space in which to prepare for another invasion. The frontier was fixed at Wadi Halfa and all posts southward were withdrawn. The safeguarding of the frontier was entrusted solely to the new, British-trained Egyptian Army, backed by a small force of British troops at Assuan until 1888 when these were withdrawn. Raids and skirmishes continued along the frontier but these served to break in the Egyptian troops for the greater test that was sure to come, and to build up their confidence in the training so patiently and devotedly instilled into them by their British officers and NCOs.

When the work of organising and training a

---

[15] An expedition led by the explorer, H.M. Stanley, was mounted in 1887 to relieve Emin Pasha from Central Africa. After many vicissitudes this was accomplished in 1889.

[16] Early in his revolt the Mahdi had called his followers 'Dervishes', literally 'poor men', but he had soon forbade this, preferring the term 'Ansar': those who consecrated themselves to God in the hope of Paradise to come. After 1885 'Dervishes' became a generic term used by the British to describe the Khalifa's followers, and will be used in this sense in the following chapters.

new Egyptian Army to defend Egypt proper was begun by Sir Evelyn Wood in 1883, there were many who maintained that the fellahin could never be made into soldiers worthy of the name. This was to overlook how abominably led and treated they had been in the old army. Besides inculcating the essentials of drill and discipline and ensuring the troops were properly clothed and armed, the first lesson the British instructors had to drive home into the Egyptian officers and NCOs was the vital importance of treating the soldier firmly but justly: that he received the pay and rations to which he was entitled; that he was allowed leave at intervals; that if sick, he was admitted to hospital; that disciplinary infringements were investigated and dealt with fairly – all basic principles of sound man-management but which had been sadly neglected or abused under the old system. Before long the fellah soldiers began to respond to the new regime, giving further proof to the old adage of there being no bad soldiers, only bad officers, and in time a remarkable feeling of mutual trust and confidence developed between the British officers and their men.

Beginning with eight infantry battalions, a cavalry regiment and two artillery batteries, the force was to grow to eighteen battalions, ten

Two types of men found in the Khalifa's ranks, the 'black' and the Arab.

squadrons of cavalry, five batteries, a camel corps and a military school for young officers. The bulk of the army was manned by indigenous Egyptian fellahin, conscripted for a period of six years, but six of the battalions, 9th–14th, were raised from black Sudanese, many of them Bazinger deserters from the Khalifa's army, of the Shilluk and Dinka tribes of the far south, enlisted on a voluntary basis for life. The difference between the two types was explained by Winston Churchill in *The River War*: 'The Egyptian was strong, patient, healthy and docile. The negro was in all these respects his inferior ... a lazy, fierce, disreputable child ... but he loved his officer and feared nothing in the world.' Though less amenable to discipline and unsuitable for garrisons in the Delta, the Sudanese battalions proved their worth on the frontier, as exemplified by the 9th Battalion who were presented with a special Colour by the Cameron Highlanders, their comrades-in-arms at Ginniss. Some of the fellah battalions were officered entirely by Egyptians, others had three or four British officers, while all the Sudanese each had five British. One man vital to the efficiency of every battalion's drill and shooting was its British colour-sergeant or sergeant instructor, immortalised by Kipling as 'Sergeant Whatsisname' who had 'a charm for making riflemen of mud'.

One of the first British officers to be appointed to the Egyptian Army in 1883 had been Herbert Kitchener who, though a sapper, had been promoted major and second-in-command of the cavalry regiment. He quickly attained a reputation as the most determined and efficient officer of the new army. Seconded for intelligence duties with the Gordon Relief Expedition, in 1886 he was appointed Governor of Suakin with the rank of colonel. Osman Digna was still very much at large and towards the end of 1887 began to threaten the fortifications of Suakin. Forbidden to use his regular garrison, Kitchener collected a force of irregulars and stormed Osman Digna's base at Handub in January 1888. However the enemy counter-attacked the indisciplined levies, in the course of which Kitchener was severely wounded, but his spirited if unauthorised conduct won him

The Khalifa's gallows in Omdurman, and some of his male and female subjects.

The Mahdist *jibbeh* or *marrakahieh*, the white shirt with coloured patches prescribed by the Mahdi to show that the wearer was pure and humble, was to be feared by his enemies, was honoured by God, and was free of all possibility of suspicion.

much admiration and, in September, the appointment of Adjutant-General of the Egyptian Army. Before he could properly assume it, the situation at Suakin had so worsened that Sir Francis Grenfell, who had followed Wood as Sirdar, took over its defence himself taking Kitchener with him as commander of a Sudanese brigade. On 20 December Grenfell routed Osman Digna in a battle which further increased Kitchener's reputation.

This was the first real test in battle of the reformed Egyptian Army, from which it emerged with honour. Eight months later it consolidated its new reputation. With the Abyssinians finally subdued, the Khalifa was again ready to attempt the invasion of Egypt. Northwards marched an army under one of the Khalifa's most able emirs, Wad-el-Nejumi, who planned to outflank Wadi Halfa by a desert march to the west and then strike in at the Nile north of Assuan. Grenfell advanced to meet him with two battalions of Egyptians, four of Sudanese, two batteries, four squadrons and the camel regiment. A British brigade was coming up, but on 3 August near Toski Grenfell saw a favourable opportunity and attacked. After some five hours' fighting the enemy was completely broken, Nejumi himself was killed and only about 800 Dervishes escaped to tell how their host had crumbled under the Egyptian musketry. None can have been more astonished at the fighting qualities of these new Egyptian soldiers than Nejumi who had led the attack on Hicks' pathetic army and the final assault on Khartoum. At Suakin the Egyptian troops had been stiffened by two British battalions — 2nd King's Own Scottish Borderers, 1st Welch Regiment — but Toski, except for a squadron of 20th Hussars, had been entirely an Egyptian Army victory. Those who six years before had poured ridicule on the idea of fellah soldiers being able to stand against Dervishes, let alone attack and conquer, had to eat their words. Furthermore the frontier had been held and would never again be threatened by invasion.

Taking time off from his office in Cairo, Kitchener had once more distinguished himself by his handling of the mounted troops. After Toski he returned to his duties as Adjutant-General in which his administrative abilities attracted as much favourable notice from his superiors as his powers of leadership in the field. In 1892 Sir Francis Grenfell retired as Sirdar, and although the able commander of the Wadi Halfa frontier force, Colonel Wodehouse, seemed the most likely successor, it was upon Kitchener that Sir Evelyn Baring's choice fell. At the early age of 42 Herbert Kitchener was

Types of the British-trained Egyptian Army. Foreground, from left: Infantry, winter and summer; British officer (mounted) and men of Sudanese battalions. Background: Cavalry and Camel Corps. The Egyptian infantry's winter dress was medium blue with cream facings, the Cavalry having light blue and white, the Artillery dark blue with scarlet. Chromolithograph after R. Simkin.

Right: An Egyptian battalion's cookhouse. Regular rations were an important feature of the British re-organisation of the Army.

appointed Commander-in-Chief of the Egyptian Army with the rank of major-general. It was a far from popular choice: his intense professionalism, his rapid promotion, his imperious manner, aloofness and lack of tact had alienated many, both in the Army and in European society in Cairo, which he held in contempt, preferring the company of the wealthier and better class of Egyptian and Turk. Nevertheless his dedication and ruthless pursuit of efficiency soon won for him, in the Army at least, respect and admiration if not affection. He had been much angered by the death of his great hero, Gordon, regarding it as England's disgrace and the evacuation of the Sudan as the policy of

scuttle. Should there be a change of heart in England about the Sudan, there was no-one who would be more eager to implement a reversal of that policy than the new Sirdar.

At the time of his appointment there seemed little likelihood of this for Gladstone and the Liberals were again in office. Three years later, however, on Gladstone's retirement, Lord Salisbury and the Conservatives were returned

Above: One of the Sudanese battalions, the backbone of the Army, marching past in review order. They are uniformed in khaki drill with blue puttees, their tarbushes having a khaki cover and the battalion's distinguishing tuft at the right side. The equipment is brown leather. On active service dark khaki jerseys replaced the tunics.

Below: The Battle of Toski, 3 August 1889, the re-vitalised Egyptian Army's first major victory over the Dervishes. The 1st Brigade are engaging the enemy before advancing to the attack. The Dervishes were eventually put to flight through the hills in the background. Watercolour sketch by Major Donne, who commanded the 10th Sudanese of that brigade.

Horatio Herbert Kitchener, appointed Sirdar of the Egyptian
Army in 1892. He commanded all Anglo-Egyptian forces in the
Sudan from 1898. Portrait by C.M. Horsfall, dated 1899.

to power, a change of government which coincided with a number of factors that began to sway public opinion away from its indifference towards Egypt and the Sudan which had set in after the failure of 1885. First there was a growing awareness and pride in the civic achievements of Baring, now Lord Cromer, in restoring Egypt to stability and prosperity during the thirteen years of his enormously capable and beneficent, if autocratic, proconsulship. In contrast was a rising indignation and anger about the state of affairs in the Sudan, as revealed by the disclosures of Slatin Pasha, once Governor of Darfur and for eleven years a prisoner in chains in Omdurman until his escape in 1895. His book, *With Fire and Sword in the Sudan*,

At left, the Austrian, Slatin Pasha, one time Governor of Darfur for the Khedive until surrendering to the Mahdi in 1884, thereafter remaining a prisoner in chains until his escape in 1895. With him is Major F.R. Wingate, Kitchener's Director of Intelligence.

vividly portrayed not only the cruelties of the Khalifa's regime, but also the internal dissensions in the country. The possibility of anarchy, leading to a power vacuum in Egypt's lost province, was not something that could be contemplated calmly by either British or Egyptian authorities in a decade when European colonisation in Africa was at its height and France, in particular, was taking a close interest in Equatoria and the Upper Nile. In the light of all these factors, thoughts started to turn towards the recovery of the Sudan.

In the event it was not France but Italy that provided the catalyst which was to translate thoughts into deeds. In March 1896 an Italian army was routed by the Abyssinians at Adowa while attempting to expand its Eritrean colony. It was feared that this humiliation of European arms might incite the Khalifa to capitalise on the Abyssinians' victory by an attack on Kassala, the advanced Italian outpost on the Sudanese border, and possibly another attempt against Suakin or even the Egyptian frontier at Wadi Halfa. In Europe Italy was a partner with Germany and Austria in the Triple Alliance which maintained the balance of power against France and Russia, the two most expansionist powers outside Europe and consequently the chief threats to the British Empire. If Italy was crushed in Africa, not only would European prestige in that area suffer but the Triple Alliance would be weakened, with benefit to France, both in Europe and where her own African aspirations were concerned. Italy was thus deserving of British support and consequently her request to Britain for help to relieve Kassala by a diversion up the Nile immediately found favour with the Government. Lord Salisbury saw in it the opportunity both to forestall further Dervish aggression in the eastern Sudan and, as he put it, 'to use the same military effort to plant the foot of Egypt rather further up the Nile.' In other words an appropriate moment to begin the reconquest of the Sudan had presented itself. Only twelve days after Adowa Cromer, Britain's Agent and Consul-General, was instructed to launch Kitchener and the Egyptian Army up the Nile to recapture the province of Dongola.

12

The Advance Begins

After a small force had been pushed southwards to occupy and establish an advanced base at Akasha, the Egyptian Army was brought up to war establishment by calling up reservists, and work began to prolong the desert railway which was to transport the troops and supplies for the campaign. By 4 June 1896 Kitchener had concentrated ten battalions, fifteen squadrons of cavalry and camel corps, and three batteries at Akasha within a day's march of the nearest Dervish position at Firket. Apart from British officers and four British-manned Maxim guns – of the 1st North Staffordshire Regiment – the entire force was Egyptian or Sudanese. Three days later, after a night approach march followed by a surprise dawn attack, from which only a third of the Dervishes managed to escape, Kitchener could report to Cromer: 'I think I can place your mind completely at rest as regards the conduct of the Egyptian troops.' True they had enjoyed a three to one advantage in men and a great superiority in weapons, but an essential part of the campaign as planned had been the forcing of an early action upon the enemy to confirm the fighting quality of the new Egyptian Army. Not only had this been proved, but fifty miles of the Nile valley was now safely in Kitchener's hands and the only organised Dervish force in the region of the frontier had been routed.

Encouragingly though the campaign had begun, it was now dogged by a series of setbacks. First an epidemic of cholera swept through the army, lowering morale and causing forty times more casualties among troops and followers than had been sustained at Firket. This was followed by freak thunder and sand storms which gravely hindered the resumed advance and swept away a twelve-mile stretch of the vital railway. By massive efforts, not least by Kitchener himself, the line was repaired

within a week and on 5 September all was ready for the final assault on Dongola. To support the land operations Kitchener had assembled a flotilla of gunboats and armed steamers, among which was the *Zafir*, one of three gunboats built in England to Kitchener's specifications and shipped out in sections to be assembled on the Nile. *Zafir* was the first to be ready and Kitchener was keen to demonstrate her capabilities and firepower to his expectant soldiers. As she pulled out into midstream with Kitchener aboard, watched by the excited soldiery assembled on the bank, there was suddenly a loud explosion and the engines stopped. The cylinder had burst and *Zafir* would be out of action until a new one could be sent up from Wadi Halfa.

Kitchener was much affected by the sorry performance of his new toy. He would have been even more infuriated could he have foretold the intentions of the enemy commander, Wad Bishara. For when he advanced on 19 September to attack the Dervish position on the east bank, he found that the night before the wily Wad Bishara had transferred his men to the west bank and slipped away upstream to an entrenchment guarding the narrows at Hafir. To force a passage Kitchener had to rely on his 1885-vintage gunboats which proved not powerful enough to silence the enemy shore batteries. Only when three artillery batteries were called up to give covering fire from the east bank were the gunboats enabled to run the gauntlet and steam on towards Dongola. Feeling his line of retreat threatened, Wad Bishara abandoned the Hafir position and retreated. Kitchener transported his troops to the west bank and, reinforced by the almost miraculous reappearance of the repaired *Zafir*, entered Dongola on 23 September, as Wad Bishara withdrew his men in the face of overwhelming

Hector MacDonald, who commanded a Sudanese brigade with great distinction throughout the reconquest of the Sudan. The son of a Highland crofter, he was commissioned from the ranks in the Afghan War, fought in the Transvaal War of 1881 and entered the Egyptian service in 1887 in command of the 11th Sudanese which he led at Toski.

strength. So as to be within convenient striking distance of the next Dervish stronghold at Abu Hamed, Kitchener pushed troops forward to Merowi and Wolseley's old base at Korti before halting all operations.

The successful Dongola expedition of 1896 gave great satisfaction in Britain, not least for the economy with which it had been conducted, and resulted in honours and awards for all concerned. Having greatly enhanced his own prestige, Kitchener at once pressed for a continuation of the advance to seize Abu Hamed and Berber without delay. Information was reaching his intelligence chief, Major Wingate, of French approaches to the Emperor of Abyssinia with a view to extending a French sphere of influence across Equatorial Africa, including the headwaters of the Nile, and that the Khalifa was also urging the Emperor to make common cause with him against the Egyptian invasion. In the light of this information Cromer was in favour of continuing operations in the Sudan but the brake on so doing, as far as the Egyptian Government was concerned, was finance. He therefore despatched Kitchener to London to seek a British contribution. This the victorious Sirdar succeeded in obtaining, to the tune of half a million pounds for expenditure on gunboats, arms, stores, transport and, most important of all, further railway construction.

The railway which had supported the Dongola expedition had stopped some fifty miles short of that town itself, but for the next phase Kitchener envisaged a far more ambitious project: the construction of a second line, some 225 miles of track, straight across the Nubian Desert from Wadi Halfa to Abu Hamed, whence it could continue in due course southwards to supply Kitchener's long-dreamed-of plan, the final advance on Khartoum. Much expert advice had been sought on this project, but because of the problems involved – the protection of the work, the feeding, fuelling and, above all, watering of the workers and locomotives in a barren and almost waterless desert, the procurement and transportation of the necessary equipment, with everything to be done within a limited budget – all those consulted, not to mention others not consulted, pronounced the scheme to be out of the question. Kitchener, however, thought otherwise, and on 1 January 1897 the construction of the Sudan Military Railway began, directed by a group of Royal Engineers subalterns under the supervision of a young French-Canadian officer of exceptional talents, Lieutenant Percy Girouard. Engines and rolling stock were bought in England, workshops were built at Wadi Halfa, the Railway Battalion of the Egyptian Army was increased in strength, and wells were sunk in the desert. What water the desert could not provide, the railway had to carry with it in huge 1500-gallon tanks. By 23 July, 103 miles of track had been completed and work was progressing at a rate of a mile and a half of line per day, but the construction gangs were now vulnerable to raiding parties from Abu Hamed, still in Dervish hands.

Major-General Hunter was therefore ordered to advance with a flying column from Merowi and surprise the Dervish garrison at Abu Hamed. Hunter was one of the most popular and distinguished officers of the Egyptian Army and the bulk of his force consisted of the predominantly Sudanese brigade of Hector MacDonald, who had been commissioned from the ranks of the Gordon Highlanders for gallantry in the Afghan War and had served with the Egyptian Army since 1887. Though it was the hottest time of the year, the column covered the 146 miles to its objective in eight days, marching mainly at night over very rough going. At dawn on 7 August, having swung wide round the Dervish position to come in from the east, MacDonald's 9th, 10th and 11th Sudanese stormed the entrenchments and fought their way through the houses of the village to the river bank. By 7.30 am it was all over and Abu Hamed, the intended railhead, was in Hunter's hands. Only a few Dervish horsemen made their escape, and such was the speed of their flight that when they met reinforcements hastening down from Berber, the latter turned back with them.

The loss of Abu Hamed and the return of his troops impelled the emir in command at Berber to seek assistance from the Emir Mahmud at Metemmeh but, when no help came, he aban-

A *noggara* or copper drum, the only type permitted by the Mahdi for his followers after forbidding the use by his troops of any instruments of Turco-Egyptian origins.

doned the town. This welcome news did not reach Hunter until 2 September, by which time he had been reinforced by the whole flotilla of gunboats which now included two more of the *Zafir* class, *Naser* and *Fateh*. He at once telegraphed for instructions.

The unforeseen abandonment of Berber placed Kitchener in a quandary. The current phase of the campaign had been designed to end with the securing of Abu Hamed as the railhead. Its defence and of the posts rearward while the line was continued to it were within the capacity of his force. Prudence and safety dictated that the original plan be adhered to. On the other hand, Berber was of strategic and moral importance, being the junction point between Khartoum and Suakin, around which Osman Digna was still active, and the chief town of the area. To occupy it now, while it was empty, could save much effort later but, being within striking distance of the main Dervish army between Metemmeh and Omdurman, it would be very vulnerable to a counter-stroke, both from that direction and from Osman Digna to the east. Moreover it would greatly extend the garrisons holding the river line back into Dongola, who would be open to an attack from Metemmeh along the route taken by the Camel Corps in 1885. Kitchener also realised that to occupy

Berber forthwith would inevitably move the campaign into its final phase – the crushing of the Khalifa at Omdurman and the recovery of Khartoum, something he had long known would require the help of British troops – before his political masters were ready for it. By recommending to Cromer the occupation of Berber and an early advance southwards he hoped, despite the risks involved, to force the issue. However Cromer, backed by Salisbury in London, though agreeing to Berber, refused to countenance any advance beyond it. His reasons were primarily based on the cost involved but to this was added a growing distrust of Kitchener's motives and, as the weeks passed, apprehension about the Sirdar's frame of mind.

In the period following the occupation of Berber, when the only activities were the continued march of the railway towards Abu Hamed and gunboat forays up the Nile, Kitchener was indeed beset by general anxieties about a massive counter-stroke from the Khalifa, as well as personal ones of being prevented from achieving his long-held ambition of avenging Gordon by his being superseded or subordinated in the command – as might well

happen if and when British troops were committed, since he was only an 'Egyptian' general. At one point he even tendered his resignation, so deeply depressed had he become, but later withdrew it. On 1 November, Girouard's first locomotive reached Abu Hamed and the Sudan Military Railway was an established fact. Nevertheless, though Kitchener continued to urge the need to attack before he was attacked, Cromer stood by his argument that funds were not available to do so. Not until over a month later was the predicament resolved. On 18 December Wingate warned Kitchener that the Khalifa was about to march on Berber with his entire army.[17] At last the men on the spot were believed and five days later Lord Salisbury authorised Cromer and Kitchener to ask for such British troops as might be required to deal with the emergency. On 4 January 1898 Kitchener was confirmed as the supreme commander of all British and Egyptian troops operating south of Assuan.

[17] Kitchener had just returned from negotiating the handover to Egypt of Kassala which, though held successfully by the Italians against Dervish attacks, had become an embarrassment to the Italian Government. On Christmas Day it was occupied by an Egyptian battalion.

13

On the Atbara

In late January the first British troops to join the Sirdar's army arrived in the Sudan. The 1st Battalions of the Royal Warwickshire and Lincolnshire Regiments and the Cameron Highlanders had been in garrison in Egypt, while the 1st Seaforth Highlanders were on their way from Malta. All were brigaded under Major-General Gatacre, known to his troops as 'Backacher', an abrasive man of restless energy and inability to delegate, who had recently made a reputation for himself during the Chitral expedition on the North-West Frontier of India. The British soldiers took the field no longer dressed in the scarlet of Tel-el-Kebir or even the grey serge of Wolseley's Nile campaign, but in the new khaki drill uniform recently authorised for all foreign service and whose yellowish-buff shade blended well with the desert sands; only the Highlanders' kilts added a touch of colour to their array. Their arms too had changed since the earlier campaigns, each infantryman now being armed with a bolt-action rifle, the Lee-Metford, fitted with a magazine containing ten rounds which afforded almost twice the rate of fire of the old Martini-Henry, with which the Egyptian Army was still armed.

While Gatacre's men were moving up, Kitchener was concentrating his Egyptian troops from their camps along the Nile around Berber

The Sirdar, booted centre, with Major-General Gatacre, back to camera wearing puttees. Officers in this campaign adopted the new Wolseley helmet.

Captain McLean and G Company, 1st Battalion Queen's Own Cameron Highlanders, on the march. The difference between McLean's and the men's helmets can be clearly seen. A blue square was worn on the side to distinguish the regiment.

and sending one brigade forward to the Nile's confluence with the River Atbara, where a fort was built in the angle. Meanwhile the Dervish army, having advanced only as far as Kerreri, ten miles north of Omdurman, was in some confusion owing to its senior emirs being unable to agree with the Khalifa as to who should actually command in the field, the Khalifa having allowed himself to be persuaded that his person was too valuable to be risked in action. Eventually, no decision having been reached, the army drifted back to Omdurman and it seemed as though the whole flurry of late December had been a false alarm. But then the young and ardent Emir Mahmud at Metemmeh, who disposed of some 20,000 men, begged for

the chance to attack Berber. Somewhat surprisingly the Khalifa agreed, and in mid-February Mahmud began to move his followers across the Nile to the east bank to join Osman Digna who had arrived at Shendi.

This was reported to Kitchener on 15 February. Mahmud's crossing was not completed until the end of the month but even then he made no move for a fortnight. The combination of the arrogant, headstrong young emir and the cautious, cunning old Osman Digna did not make for unity of purpose. Eventually, on 13 March, the Dervish host was observed by the gunboats to be heading north. Seemingly unaware or uncaring of the strength and dispositions of the Anglo-Egyptian army, Mahmud appeared bent on a frontal assault. Kitchener immediately ordered a concentration just north of Atbara fort which was completed by the 16th. Two days later Mahmud changed his mind and was seen heading north-east away from the

Nile towards the Atbara, obviously with the intention of approaching Berber from a flank. Leaving one Egyptian battalion to guard Atbara fort, Kitchener marched all his force across the desert to intercept, reaching Hudi on the Atbara river late on the 20th. Poor though Mahmud's information about his enemy may have been hitherto, the advance of 14,000 men of all arms could hardly escape his notice and he again altered course, now due east to strike the Atbara at Nakheila. This move put Berber even further out of his reach, for to outflank Kitchener from Nakheila would require a wide sweep out into the desert for which he had neither water nor supplies. Kitchener's steady advance from the north-west was protecting Berber without a shot being fired. On the next day a flank march was put even more out of the question by Kitchener's arrival at Ras-el-Hudi, only twenty miles from the point reached by the Dervishes. All that remained to Mahmud was to entrench his army behind a zariba with his back to the river. He had been completely out-manoeuvred, but his precise whereabouts were as yet unknown to Kitchener.

In the last week of March, while Kitchener's troops, particularly the British, sweltered and suffered in the dusty camp at Ras-el-Hudi, the Egyptian cavalry under Lieutenant-Colonel Broadwood daily rode out to try and locate the Dervish army. Among the British squadron leaders was a Captain Douglas Haig, lately transferred from the 7th Hussars and within twenty years the commander of nearly two million men: an ambitious and thoughtful soldier, he had recently graduated from the Staff College and, at the age of thirty-six, was about to see action for the first time. Haig soon found that, 'although the pluck of the Egyptian cavalryman is right enough', reconnaissance was not his strong point, 'the outpost service being carelessly done (and) the eyesight of the Egyptian can't be relied on.' The going and visibility along the Atbara's banks were difficult enough owing to the dense scrub and palm trees, and in addition Broadwood had only 800 troopers to penetrate Mahmud's cavalry screen of some 4000 Baggara horse, who were altogether more bold and skilful. Not until 30 March, when General Hunter led a reconnaissance in force, was the position and extent of Mahmud's zariba finally discovered.

A desert bivouac made from blankets and groundsheets.

145

Deserters brought before Wingate revealed some idea of Mahmud's numbers, that his food supplies, though short, were not yet exhausted, and that inactivity was breeding discontent; the latter was likely to increase when and if the Dervishes heard of a raid made on Shendi by the gunboats under Commander Keppel RN, in which large numbers of Mahmud's followers' women were taken prisoner and brought to Atbara, where they appeared more than willing to transfer their allegiance to the delighted Sudanese soldiery. Despite these promising signs, however, Kitchener was suddenly seized by a fit of indecision, a strange weakness in such a dominant personality but one that was to afflict him at crucial moments throughout his later career, – particularly over the Dardanelles in 1915 when Secretary of State for War. Should he attack the zariba, with the considerable loss such a course might entail, or wait for Mahmud to attack him, with the risk that he might not do so and merely withdraw unscathed? Faced with conflicting advice from Gatacre advocating an assault and Hunter advising delay, Kitchener telegraphed to Cromer who, devoid of military experience in the field, sought advice from London. The general consensus from Cairo and London counselled delay, but before this was received Hunter changed his mind and Kitchener decided to take the offensive. To some extent this was forced on him as the heat and state of the camp was starting to affect the health of the British brigade.

On 4 April the whole army marched to a new camp four miles nearer the enemy and the next day the cavalry went out for a final reconnaissance. At first the zariba seemed deserted but suddenly the Baggara horse appeared, threatening both flanks while Mahmud's few guns opened fire from the entrenchments. Broadwood ordered a retirement, but as the squadrons went back two successive attacks were made on the Horse Artillery and Maxim battery in the centre. Any failure in reconnaissance was now vindicated by a spirited action of the flanking squadrons which, well led by their British officers, charged home and checked the Baggara by quickly dismounting, then opening fire with their carbines to hold off any pursuit.

By the evening of the 7th all was ready for the assault next day on the zariba, now only some seven miles off. Just before sunset the Anglo-Egyptian army paraded and marched off, each of the four infantry brigades in a huge square, one behind the other, the British leading. The cavalry and artillery were to follow on later. During the march the army was rested and watered in the middle of the night, and shortly after four o'clock the whole mass halted on a plateau to the north of, and some 900 yards from the camp fires marking the enemy's position. Here in silence the brigades waited for dawn while below them the Dervishes slept.

As the sun came up over the desert the battalions stood up and moved into their attack formations, the whole force arrayed in an arc along the ridge just behind the crest. On the left, the British, with the Camerons in front, all eight companies in line, and behind them from left to right the Royal Warwicks, Seaforth and Lincolns, each battalion in column of companies. In the centre, MacDonald's brigade, his three Sudanese battalions in line each with three companies forward and three in support, with the 2nd Egyptians behind in column. On the right, Maxwell's brigade, the 12th, 13th and 14th Sudanese in line, each with four companies forward and two in support, with the 8th Egyptians in reserve. To the left rear of the Warwicks stood Lewis's all-Egyptian brigade of three battalions in square, guarding the transport and water camels, with the Camel Corps on its right. The guns and Maxims were deployed along the line, while out on the far left, guarding the British flank, was the Egyptian cavalry. Some 12,000 men in all, twenty-four guns, four Maxims and a rocket detachment. As the troops took up their positions, a description of their objective was noted down by the war correspondent, G.W. Steevens: 'The usual river fringe of grey-green palms meeting the usual desert fringe of yellow-grey mimosa. And the smoke-grey line in front of it all must be their famous zariba. Up from it rolled a nimbus of

1st Battalion, Seaforth Highlanders forcing an entry into the zariba at the Atbara, 8 April 1898. Drawing by R. Caton Woodville after a sketch by Captain Sir H. Rawlinson.

dust, as if they were still busy at entrenching; before its right centre fluttered half a dozen flags, white and pale blue, yellow and pale chocolate.'

At 6.20 the first Egyptian gun fired and in seconds all four batteries were in action, methodically pounding the interior of the zariba from front to rear, from side to side, with shell and shrapnel, while the fizzing projectiles of the rocket detachment sailed down among the scrub and palms starting fires. At one moment a mass of Baggara horse galloped out from cover as though to charge the left flank, but two Maxims, backed by the Egyptian cavalry, quickly deterred any onset. For an hour and twenty minutes the bombardment rained down on the Dervishes hidden in their trenches and then the guns fell silent. The waiting infantry stood up, the lines were adjusted, and the bugles sounded the advance. The whole army,

some 1500 yards from flank to flank, marched forward as one man, the fixed bayonets flashing in the sun above the ranks of khaki helmets and tarbushes. Over the crunch of massed boots and shouted orders rose the high scream of the Highlanders' pipes, the rattling drums and shrilling fifes of the English battalions and the raucous brass of the Sudanese. The guns had limbered up and were rolling forward with the infantry, ready to swing into action if need be, but the covering fire was now all musketry as the leading battalions halted at intervals on the bugle and fired section volleys into the zariba. Then on again at the same steady pace, the ranks aligned, each man's gaze fixed to his front, wondering when and how the enemy would react. The Sudanese had faced and overcome Dervishes before, but for most of the British infantrymen this was their first action.

The distance narrowed. Suddenly, at about 300 yards, the zariba blazed fire, 'the bullets,' recorded Steevens, 'swishing and lashing like rain on a pond'. Among the Camerons men began to fall but the files closed up and the

The Emir Mahmud after the Atbara guarded by soldiers of the 10th Sudanese who captured him in the zariba. The British officer is probably Major Nason, the battalion commander.

THE ATBARA CAMPAIGN, MARCH–APRIL 1898

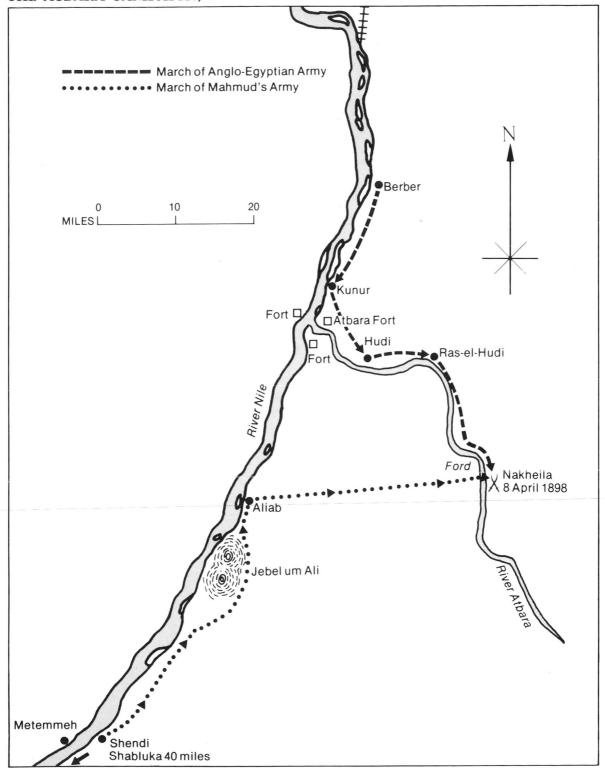

- - - - - March of Anglo-Egyptian Army
· · · · · · March of Mahmud's Army

N

0   10   20
MILES

Berber

Kunur

Fort

Atbara Fort

Hudi

Ras-el-Hudi

Fort

River Nile

Ford

Nakheila
8 April 1898

Aliab

Jebel um Ali

River Atbara

Metemmeh

Shendi
Shabluka 40 miles

advancing line of swinging kilts drew closer and closer, the regular volleys breaking into independent fire as the leading ranks strove to drive the enemy from their barricade with rapid musketry. Soon it was reached, a loose hedge of dry camel-thorn. The lines halted. 'Pull it away,' someone shouted. Through the gaps thus easily made the assault columns poured, fighting their way with bullet and bayonet through the inner stockade and maze of trenches and rifle-pits with which the thick undergrowth was honeycombed. On the right the black battalions swarmed over the thorn hedge as though it were no more than long grass, their extended formations enabling them to press on more quickly than the British columns, though suffering heavier casualties in their headlong rush. Particularly hard-hit were the 11th Sudanese who encountered the fiercest resistance at Mahmud's inner redoubt, but they and the 10th stormed into it and triumphantly dragged the Dervish commander from his hideout. Some of the Dervishes held their ground till they were killed, others ran but only to take up another position further back. Any who tried to break out to the flanks were shot down by the Warwicks, whose advance took the east side in enfilade, while Maxwell's brigade hemmed them in on the far flank; but the brunt of winkling out the hidden defenders fell upon the Seaforth, the Lincolns and MacDonald's men. At length the palm trees and scrub thinned and the victorious, sweating infantry reached the river bank. 'Across the trickle of water,' wrote Steevens, 'the quarter-mile of dry sand-bed was a flypaper with scrambling spots of black. The pursuers thronged the bank in double line, and in two minutes the paper was still black-spotted, only the spots scrambled no more.'

At 8.25 the bugles blew 'Cease Fire' and the battle was over. The Baggara horse, the wily Osman Digna among them, had made good their escape, but Mahmud was a prisoner and his host was destroyed or dispersed. Well over 2000 Dervish dead were found within the zariba. Hundreds of the Jehadia black infantry who, unlike the Arab horse, had bravely stood their ground, were taken prisoner and later were quite content to be enlisted in the Sudanese battalions. The Anglo-Egyptian losses were 80 killed and 479 wounded of whom some later died from their wounds. The hardest-hit British battalion was the Camerons who lost three officers and 57 other casualties. The five Egyptian battalions' losses of only 14 men, in contrast to the 375 casualties sustained by the six Sudanese, showed how much reliance was placed on the latter.

Weary but triumphant the Anglo-Egyptian army made its way back to the Nile, there to go into summer quarters around Berber and Atbara fort to await reinforcements and make preparations for the final phase of the campaign. A significant defeat had been inflicted on one of the Khalifa's most favoured lieutenants and his forces broken. Kitchener lost no opportunity in impressing this fact upon the people of Berber by his Roman triumph of a victory parade through the town, with a fettered Mahmud forced to follow in the wake of his conqueror's white horse, as the bands played and the excited crowds reviled the vanquished Emir. Two hundred miles up-river to the south, the Khalifa sat in his palace at Omdurman, defiantly bidding his horde to prepare to resist the invaders. To his followers he displayed unbounded confidence in the outcome but perhaps, when he heard his spies' reports of what was coming against him, his bravado began to conceal a creeping shadow of apprehension.

Opoosite below: Victors of the Atbara. Privates Watt, Smith and Macdonald of the Cameron Highlanders. Yellowish-brown khaki is now universally worn instead of the grey of the 1884–85 campaign.

Opposite above: Cameron and Seaforth Highlanders burying their dead after the battle. The Seaforth, with a white line in their kilts, wore a small white hackle behind the badge on the left side of the helmet.

14

Kitchener's Triumph

While the victors of the Atbara broiled in their summer camps or, if officers, went on leave to Cairo (even in some cases to England) the extra troops needed for a really decisive and final blow at the Khalifa were moving south. Commander Keppel's flotilla of seven gunboats was increased by three more of the most modern design, *Melik*, *Sudan* and *Sheikh*, each driven by a screw instead of a stern-wheel, and mounting four guns and four Maxims, giving a total riverborne armament of thirty-six guns and twenty-fours Maxims. The land-based artillery was augmented to forty-four guns and twenty Maxims by the arrival of another Egyptian battery, the 32nd and 37th Field Batteries, Royal Artillery, whose fourteen guns included six 5-inch howitzers and two 40-pounder siege guns, and additional British-manned Maxims of the Royal Artillery and 1st Royal Irish Fusiliers.

To Hunter's Egyptian infantry division was added a fourth, all-Egyptian brigade under Colonel Collinson, so that he now disposed of ten Egyptian battalions and six Sudanese. General Gatacre was promoted from brigade to divisional commander, for the seasoned British battalions of the Atbara, now under command of Brigadier-General Wauchope, were joined by Brigadier-General Lyttleton's 2nd Brigade. This formation included not only two Line battalions from Cairo, the 1st Northumberland Fusiliers and 1st Lancashire Fusiliers, but also the 1st Grenadier Guards from Gibraltar and 2nd Rifle Brigade from Malta. The experienced eye of the correspondent, Steevens, was impressed by the Fusiliers who stood comparison with what he called 'the splendid sun-dried battalions of the First Brigade', but his first sight of the Guards and Rifles, unacclimatised as they were, was hardly up to their reputation of 'crack' regiments, and within days of their ar-

rival, many were in the field hospital with sunstroke.

Inevitably the arrival of the newcomers drew caustic remarks from the old hands, but none more so than those which greeted the four squadrons of the only British cavalry of the force, the 21st Lancers, who came ashore from barges looking the worse for wear after their journey. This, the junior regiment of all British cavalry, had been formed less than forty years before and had never been in action, a misfortune that had given rise to a popular witticism that its regimental motto was 'Thou shalt not kill'. The need to correct this slur at any cost greatly preoccupied the regiment's Commanding Officer, Colonel Martin, who concealed a slow mind and his inexperience behind an aggressive and superior manner. Among his officers was one from a far older and more distinguished regiment, whose poor view of the 21st was matched by the dislike he inspired in his fellow subalterns: Lieutenant Winston Spencer Churchill of the 4th Hussars. He proposed combining his duties as troop officer with those of correspondent for *The Morning Post*; already his journalistic criticisms of a recent North-West Frontier campaign had aroused furious resentment within the Army and, if this was not enough, his presence with the Nile Expeditionary Force had been obtained against Kitchener's express wishes through the blandishments of his charming mother, Lady Randolph Churchill, upon anyone who might be useful from the Prince of Wales downwards.

So, throughout August, by rail, steamer and march route, the guns, cavalry, infantry, supporting services, animal transport and followers all came up the Nile to the new concentration area at Wad Hamed, only fifty-eight miles from Omdurman, until the whole expeditionary force, the largest ever deployed in the

Maxim gun detachment of the 1st Royal Irish Fusiliers which joined Kitchener before the final advance. The gun mules are in the rear with Egyptian muleteers.

Sudan was assembled: 8200 British, 17,600 Egyptians and Sudanese, 2469 horses and 4649 mules, camels and donkeys. Not only was it a large and well-supplied force but it was equipped with the most up-to-date technology of warfare — magazine rifles, machine-guns, howitzers, heliographs and searchlights. On 24 August the great and final advance began, as the Egyptian Division led off up the west bank of the Nile.

Meanwhile the Khalifa, having given orders for the fortification of his capital and the mobilisation of every man fit to bear arms, withdrew behind the protection of his 2000-strong Taaisha bodyguard and the 14-foot-high stone wall encircling his palace, wherein the grandest appurtenances were a brass bed, his two bath taps, also brass but otherwise useless, and a harem of 400 women to satisfy his not inconsiderable appetites. Only there did he feel secure, not so much from Kitchener, whose numbers were little more than a third of his, but from the uncertain loyalties of some of his subordinates. There, between the mosque and the great yellow dome of the Mahdi's tomb, he communed with the spirit of his mighty predecessor, seeking guidance whether to sally forth and conquer on the plain of Kerreri, as the Mahdi had allegedly forecast, or sit behind his fortifications and make the infidel fight through the streets and houses of the town.

The Khalifa's likely course of action was also being pondered by Kitchener. From the 28th the whole army marched in one huge fighting formation, the British Division on the left, the Egyptians stretching out into the desert, the

153

Opposite: 1st Battalion, Grenadier Guards entraining at Cairo station before moving south.

The Mahdi's tomb at Omdurman, showing the damage done by the bombardment of 1 September.

front screened by the cavalry with patrols far ahead, while the Camel Corps watched the open, right flank and the gunboats patrolled the river on the left. Little had been seen of the Dervishes, other than some tracks in the sand, and many in the British regiments wondered, as each day's march brought them closer to Omdurman, whether there would be a battle at all. The more experienced officers of the Egyptian Army, however, thought otherwise. Ahead lay the Kerreri Hills, reaching for some two miles out into the desert at right angles to the river, the last high ground covering the approaches to Omdurman. From a distance the 21st Lancers had spotted Dervishes forward of the hills but these had ridden off. Until the position was reconnoitred, it would not be known if it was held in strength, or whether the

Opposite: The Queen's Company, Grenadier Guards aboard a river steamer going up the Nile. The regimental red and blue cockades on the helmets, the neck curtains (not worn by the Highland battalions) and spine pads are clearly visible.

Khalifa was holding back his masses to defend the city itself, which could prove a lengthy and costly business for the attackers. To deter the Khalifa from such a course, Kitchener decided to give his adversary a demonstration of the fire power of modern artillery upon closely-packed, mud-built dwellings.

On 1 September, as the infantry continued to march southwards and the cavalry rode out to scout the Kerreri Hills and the plain beyond, the gunboats steamed up towards Omdurman while the howitzers of the 37th Battery were ferried across to the east bank, where a site within range of the town had been seized by friendly irregulars under Major Stuart-Wortley. At eleven o'clock the gunboats opened fire on the Khalifa's forts, silencing them one by one with shell and Maxim fire, and afterwards switching to the great wall within the town, pounding away until sections of it began to crumble. At 1.30 the howitzers came into action, their high explosive shells roaring over the river to burst amid clouds of smoke and dust around the prominent dome of the Mahdi's tomb. With the third shot the pointed top disappeared and, the range thus assured, the ensuing salvoes achieved more direct hits before moving on to other targets. As the explosions and destruction mounted, as the people gazed with horror at the damage to the sacred tomb, the Khalifa abandoned the idea of fighting in the streets and ordered every man still in the town to join the army already forming on the plain outside.

In the meantime the 21st Lancers, with the Egyptian cavalry on their right, having found the Kerreri Hills deserted, had ridden on another three miles to the next ridge which ran up from the river to a solitary black hill, a mile and a half inland. From this, the Jebel Surgham, the Lancer patrols caught their first sight of Omdurman and, to the left and slightly further away among palm trees at the confluence of the two Niles, the ruined palace of Khartoum where Gordon had died thirteen years before. To the right, and about four miles distant, Winston Churchill noticed, 'a long black line with white spots'. The cavalry patrols edged forward until: 'Suddenly the whole black line, which seemed

Maxim guns in position between the left battalion of Maxwell's brigade and the right battalion of the British Division.

to be a zariba, began to move. It was made of men not bushes. Behind it other immense masses and lines of men appeared . . . Four miles from end to end, and in five great divisions, this mighty army advanced, and swiftly. Between the masses horsemen galloped continually. Before them many patrols dotted the plain, above them waved hundreds of banners, and the sun, glinting on perhaps forty thousand hostile spear-points, spread a sparkling cloud. It was, perhaps, the impression of a lifetime, nor do I expect ever again to see such an awe-inspiring and formidable sight.'[18]

Churchill was sent back to report to Kitchener – an encounter he did not relish. The Sirdar by this time, around midday, was just arriving with the infantry at the village of El Egeiga on the river bank just south of the Kerreri Hills. Shortly afterwards news of the

continued Dervish advance was flashed by heliograph from the top of Jebel Surgham. It looked as though there might be a battle that afternoon, so the infantry, who had already begun to construct a camp site and zariba around the village, were ordered to re-position themselves further out in a wide arc to permit more space for the siting of the artillery and deployment of reserves. There was very little scrub around to make a new zariba, and what there was, was taken by the British Division, so the Egyptian brigades had to scrape out a shallow trench. Urgently the work went on under the blistering sun but then came reports that the enemy had halted. All afternoon the cavalry patrols kept watch, but by the time the sun went down and they headed back to the army, the great mass out in the desert had made no move. One question now preoccupied every man within the zariba: would they wait for daylight or would they come soon, in the night?

Guarded by double sentries and officers' patrols, while the gunboats' searchlights swept the silent desert, each man rested, his rifle at his

[18] Written on 5 September to the proprietor of *The Morning Post*.

THE BATTLE OF OMDURMAN, 2 SEPTEMBER 1898

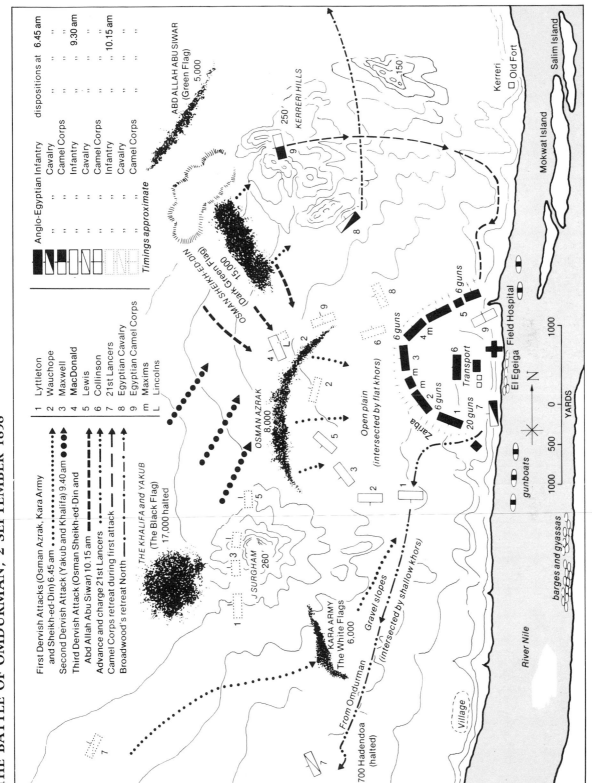

First Dervish Attacks (Osman Azrak, Kara Army and Sheikh-ed-Din) 6.45 am ••••••••

Second Dervish Attack (Yakub and Khalifa) 9.40am ●●●●

Third Dervish Attack (Osman Sheikh-ed-Din and Abd Allah Abu Siwar) 10.15am ▬ ▬ ▬

Advance and charge 21st Lancers •—•—•—

Camel Corps retreat during first attack —·—·—·

Broadwood's retreat North —— ——

THE KHALIFA and YAKUB
(The Black Flag)
17,000 halted

KARA ARMY
6,000
The White Flags

J SURGHAM
260'

Gravel slopes

From Omdurman

(intersected by shallow khors)

700 Hadendoa
(halted)

River Nile

Village

barges and gyassas

YARDS

1000   500   0   500   1000

N

gunboats

El Egeiga

Field Hospital

Transport

Zariba

20 guns

6 guns

6 guns

6 guns

6 guns

6 guns

Open plain
(intersected by flat khors)

OSMAN AZRAK
8,000

OSMAN SHEIKH-ED-DIN
(Dark Green Flag)
15,000

ABD ALLAH ABU SIWAR
(Green Flag)
5,000

KERRERI HILLS

250'

150'

Kerreri

□ Old Fort

Mokwat Island

Salim Island

dispositions at   **6.45 am**

Anglo-Egyptian Infantry   "   "   "
    "   Cavalry   "   "   "
    "   Camel Corps   "   "   "
    "   Infantry   "   "   **9.30 am**
    "   Cavalry   "   "   "
    "   Camel Corps   "   "   "
    "   Infantry   "   "   **10.15 am**
    "   Cavalry   "   "   "
    "   Camel Corps   "   "   "

Timings approximate

1   Lyttleton
2   Wauchope
3   Maxwell
4   MacDonald
5   Lewis
6   Collinson
7   21st Lancers
8   Egyptian Cavalry
9   Egyptian Camel Corps
m   Maxims
L   Lincolns

Above: Sketch made from a gunboat, of Kitchener's position around El Egeiga on the Nile. In the right foreground Egyptian cavalry are approaching the right wing held by Lewis's Egyptian brigade, beyond which can be seen the village, baggage animals and field hospitals. On the skyline, centre, is the Jebel Surgham. Drawn by H.C. Seppings-Wright, war artist for the *Illustrated London News*.

Below: Reserve companies of 1st Grenadier Guards awaiting the Dervish attack at Omdurman. This battalion was the first to open fire. The Nile can just be seen above the men's helmets.

side. Some slept without a care, others dozed fitfully, waking at every small sound; a few found sleep impossible and lay awake, contemplating what lay ahead, the savage onrush with spear and sword which even now might be creeping upon the zariba. Behind them the transport animals were restless, while out in front the moonlight played tricks upon the watchful sentries. Five miles away across the sand, once the thudding drums and moaning war-horns were silent, the Dervish horde watched fearfully the sweeping eyes of the searchlights, while the Khalifa and his emirs argued over reports that it was they who would be attacked in darkness. Thus the long hours slowly passed, each army knowing that soon all its courage and resolution would be put to the test.

At half-past three, an hour and a half before dawn, the Anglo-Egyptian army was silently roused and stood to arms, watching and waiting in the desert's chill as the darkness slowly began to pale. Half an hour later the suspense was broken as the bugles and trumpets blared out 'Reveille', the British battalions' drums and fifes joining in to lift the spirits. Not long afterwards, at the first hint of dawn, the cavalry trotted out, an Egyptian squadron under Captain Baring to the Jebel Surgham, the 21st Lancers to the ridge between Surgham and the river, and the rest of the Egyptian cavalry, with its horse artillery battery and the Camel Corps, towards the Kerreri Hills. Within the zariba, the growing light revealed the whole semi-circle of the infantry defenders: on the extreme left, or south end, the Rifle Brigade with guns and Maxims between its companies, its line being continued by the two Fusilier battalions and the Grenadiers; another group of Maxims, then the 1st British Brigade, Warwicks, Camerons, Seaforth and Lincolns; in the centre the two predominantly Sudanese brigades of Maxwell and MacDonald with guns and Maxims interspersed; and on the extreme right, completing the arc back to the river bank, Lewis's four Egyptian battalions. Each battalion had two companies held back in support, the remainder all in line in double rank. Behind the fighting line, Collinson's Egyptian brigade was in reserve in front of the transport and the two divisional hospitals. On the river, in rear of the army, the gunboats were getting up steam. All eyes were to the front, watching for the first galloper from the scouting cavalry. Would the Dervishes come, or would it be an advance on Omdurman?

At about 6.15, as George Steevens later described, 'a trooper rose out of the dimness behind the Jebel Surgham, grew larger and plainer, spurred violently up to the line and inside. A couple more were silhouetted across our front. Then the electric whisper came racing down the line; they were coming. The Lancers came in on the left; the Egyptian mounted troops (Baring's squadron) drew like a curtain across us from left to right. As they passed a flicker of white flags began to extend and fill the front in their place. The noise of something began to creep in upon us; it cleared and divided into the tap of drums and the faraway surf of raucous war cries. A shiver of expectancy thrilled along our army, and then a sigh of content. They were coming on. Allah help them! they were coming on'.

Across the open plain to the right of Surgham a mass of some 8000 warriors with white flags drew closer by the minute. From the river side of the hill more white flags appeared as another force came into view. Beyond the first body was an even larger mass of about 20,000 under green flags. It was soon clear that the first two divisions were heading straight for the zariba, having peeled off from the larger mass which was making for the Kerreri Hills where Broadwood and the Egyptian mounted troops still waited. At 6.25, at a range of 2700 yards, the 32nd Field Battery opened fire, followed almost immediately by the Egyptian guns. As the shells exploded, the dense masses seemed to shudder but continued to roll forward like a huge wave. The gunboats joined in but still they came. Behind the zariba, the front rank kneeling, the rear standing, the British infantry checked their loading and set their sights. At 2000 yards the Grenadier Guards opened fire with section volleys, followed by the Warwicks, the Highlanders and Lincolns, and — as the enemy veered left away from the British fire

— by Maxwell's Sudanese. 'We blazed away into the brown of them at long ranges', wrote Lieutenant Hodgson of the Lincolns later, but the firing was unhurried and deliberate, the rifle sights carefully adjusted as the range decreased. Under the pitiless volleys, the rattling Maxim fire and the exploding shells the valiant Dervishes were rent apart but still they struggled forward. As their banners fell, so they were picked up and carried onwards, only to fall again. The Lee-Metfords grew too hot to handle, the Maxims boiled over but, as Steevens observed, 'they came very fast and they came very straight; and then presently they came no further'. Few of the Dervishes got closer than 800 yards to the British rifles, perhaps 500 yards to the Sudanese with their obsolete Martini-Henrys, though one or two heroic or lucky spirits came to within a furlong of the continuous muzzle flashes before they were finally struck down.

The British soldiers were doing the job they were trained and paid to do, but few were unmoved by the slaughter they were inflicting. Hodgson remarked afterwards how sorry he felt for such 'cool and brave men', while a soldier of the Warwicks said, 'those black chaps knew how to fight and how to die.' After forty minutes action the British Division ceased fire. The first attack had been demolished, but not a Dervish had run, and the few that were left retired 'with a haughty stalk of offended dignity'. A group of enemy riflemen took cover not far in front of the Camerons and opened fire, causing casualties in the two Highland battalions which, unlike the Sudanese in their trenches found the zariba no protection against bullets. After a while, however, the enemy were dislodged by artillery fire.

The men who made this attack, estimated at between 12–14,000, were Ibrahim al Khalil's Kara Army on the right wing and Osman Azrak's followers supported by part of the Mulazamin, who had been detached for this frontal assault from the command of the Khalifa's eldest, but inexperienced son, Osman

Dervish dead in front of the zariba.

Sheikh-ed-Din. The latter had been ordered to assail the weaker right flank of the Anglo-Egyptian position with his 15,000 warriors, while the 5000 men of the Khalifa's second-in-command, Ali Wad Helu, were to remain hidden in reserve behind the Kerreri Hills under their field commander, Abd Allah Abu Siwar. Should the frontal and flank attacks fail, and the Sirdar's army advance into the open, the concealed 5000 were to be hurled at its right flank, while the Khalifa's main reserve of 17,000 under his brother, Yakub, lurking behind Surgham, would attack its left. By 7.30 Osman Azrak's first frontal attempt had failed but Osman Sheikh-ed-Din had been diverted.

On the Kerreri Hills, Broadwood had dismounted four of his eight companies of Camel Corps to form a firing line, supported by the horse artillery and two Maxims, with the other four guarding the camels, and his nine cavalry squadrons in reserve. He had been ordered to deter any Dervish move through or round the hills against Lewis's Egyptians on the extreme right. However, as he watched the attack develop on the plain below, he soon perceived that coming against his small force was no subsidiary pincer movement, but the masses of Osman Sheikh-ed-Din's Mulazamin under their dark green flags, while the bright green flags of Abd Allah Abu Siwar were swinging round the north-west end of the hills, a movement which could imperil his own right and rear. He immediately despatched a report to Kitchener, who sent back that he was to retire at once upon the zariba. But Broadwood, appreciating that the Dervish pursuit of such a retreat would bring the enemy straight down on Lewis's weak brigade, decided to make a fighting withdrawal northwards, in the hope of enticing the Dervish left wing away from the zariba.

He set his squadrons in motion accordingly as the dismounted Camel Corps and guns opened fire on the waves of warriors surging up the slopes. Though the fire of so few could have little effect upon such a host, the camel men bravely held their ground until the nearest enemy were 300 yards away, then raced back to their camels. They reached them safely and mounted, but the ground was so broken and

jagged that their progress down the slopes was slower than that of the yelling Dervishes now in hot pursuit. The horse battery delayed limbering up until the last possible moment but lost two guns in the process. Broadwood realised there was no hope of taking the Camel Corps with him northwards and ordered its commander to make best speed for the zariba, while the cavalry squadrons tried to delay the pursuers with dismounted fire. But so numerous were the enemy and so rapid their onrush – with thousands hurtling towards the river to cut the line of retreat – that if the Camel Corps which was now encumbered with wounded was to stand a chance of survival, Broadwood saw he would have to risk his squadrons in what might well prove to be a suicidal charge over broken ground into the thick of the enemy – even assuming that his Egyptian troopers would follow. He formed line to do so, but at that moment the gunboats *Melik* and *Abu Klea* came to the rescue, opening fire with guns and Maxims.

The effect of this sudden intervention upon the headlong, triumphant pursuers was devastating. Those in front fell in tangled heaps, causing the mass behind to waver and hold back. In the breathing-space afforded them, the sorely-tried but still cohesive Camel Corps made a dash for the zariba and safety. Baulked of their prey and still hammered by the gunboats, the Dervishes wheeled away northwards after the still intact cavalry. Slowly Broadwood fell back by stages, covering his movement by dismounted carbine and artillery fire, each bound drawing Osman Sheikh-ed-Din further away from the main battle. After he had gone some three miles, Broadwood launched a squadron in a successful charge against the leading Dervish horsemen, thus managing to break contact. Then, leaving the bulk of Sheikh-ed-Din's foot soldiers far out in the desert, he led his men back in a wide loop to the river, from where he was able to return to the zariba under the gunboats' protection, riding in at about 9 o'clock.

Following this useful action by the Egyptian cavalry against vastly superior numbers, the opportunity arose for the 21st Lancers to perform an equally valuable service. A second frontal attack had met the same fate as the first, and with the Dervish left apparently drawn away, it seemed to Kitchener – as far as he could judge from his command post in the zariba – that only broken and fugitive bodies of enemy now lay between his army and Omdurman. The time was therefore ripe for an advance before any other unbroken formations that might still be about could get back to Omdurman and force him to fight in the streets. First, however, he needed to be sure that the unseen ground between the Surgham ridge and the city was clear. Colonel Martin, thirsting for action, was delighted to be told to take his Lancers forward and reconnoitre. The chance for his regiment to disprove its somewhat inglorious reputation had at last arrived.

While the infantry prepared to march, the Lancers rode out behind their forward patrols, in Churchill's words, 'a great square block of ungainly brown figures and little horses, hung all over with water-bottles, saddle-bags, picketing-gear, tins of bully beef, all jolting and jangling together; the polish of peace gone; soldiers without glitter; horsemen without grace; but still a regiment of light cavalry in active operation against the enemy.' After crossing the ridge, the presence of fugitives heading for the city and small scattered groups on the plain was signalled back to Kitchener who replied: 'Annoy them as far as possible on their flank and head them off if possible from Omdurman.'

The patrols continued forward until one heading south-west beyond Surgham reported to Martin a line of some 700 blue-clad Dervishes waiting motionless near a shallow watercourse, or *khor*, ahead. Martin wheeled his regiment to the left to approach this body from a flank but, as the Lancers rode across the enemy front in column of troops, the Dervishes suddenly opened a rapid rifle-fire which brought down several men and horses. At once Martin ordered: 'Right wheel into line!' As his trumpeter sounded the call, the whole sixteen troops wheeled into one long line, the lances came down and the 21st charged for the first time in war. There were only about 200 yards to cover and it looked as if the few tribesmen, even with rifles, would be simply bowled over by the galloping hooves of 300 horses or transfixed by the lance-points. Like Cardigan at Balaclava, Colonel Martin, well ahead of his regiment, did not even draw his sword. But before half the distance had been covered he saw, too late, that he had been gulled. Before him was not a shallow depression with some scattered riflemen, but a deep, twenty-foot-wide gulley packed with 2000 white-clad spearmen and swordsmen, crouching twelve deep in a line as long as that of the charging Lancers. Unknown to the thrusting Martin, this cunning ambush had been deployed by the old warrior, Osman Digna, as soon as scouts on top of Surgham had reported the Lancers' advance. It was too late to change course and, spurring their horses, the Lancers crashed at full gallop into the khor.

As Churchill wrote, 'the collision was prodigious. Nearly thirty Lancers, men and horses, and at least two hundred Arabs were overthrown'. But as the cavalrymen strove to keep their seats, or remount if they had fallen, the Dervishes sprang at them, hamstringing the horses, slashing at reins and stirrup leathers, every blow designed to bring the riders to the ground where they could be quickly butchered. For about two minutes it was a hacking, stabbing struggle of sword and lance against spear and sword. Then the Lancers were through, riding on for two hundred yards where they rallied and faced about, ready to charge again. The cost had been heavy: out of a regimental strength of just 300, five officers, 65 men and 119 horses had been killed or wounded. When Lieutenant Smyth looked at his battered troop, he saw 'blood, blood, blood everywhere ... horses and men smothered'. The slashed nose, cheeks and mouth of a troop sergeant flapped horribly amid bubbles of blood as he tried to shout orders at his men.

Colonel Martin, miraculously unharmed, had got the charge he and his officers had craved for but, as he surveyed his lacerated regiment and the still unbroken Dervishes, even he realised the folly of a second charge. Wheeling off to a flank he dismounted two squadrons and opened fire with carbines into the khor. So effective was this that within a few minutes the enemy broke off the fight and made off towards

1st Battalion Royal Warwickshire Regiment resting after the first attack. This battalion had a red helmet flash. The zariba can be seen in the background.

Surgham, still in good order. The charge had been costly, had failed to inflict heavy casualties but at least had demonstrated there was nothing wrong with the courage and discipline of the 21st Lancers. Three of their number, Captain Kenna, Lieutenant de Montmorency and Private Byrne, were later awarded the Victoria Cross for saving fallen comrades from certain death. What it had not accomplished was the task given it by Kitchener, a thorough reconnaissance of the ground beyond Surgham. This failure was about to have its effect on the crisis of the main battle.

By 9.15, while the Lancers were in action, the infantry brigades had advanced out of the zariba and wheeled southwards heading for Omdurman. The two British brigades, supposedly in echelon but actually in line with one another, were approaching the ridge between Surgham and the river. Echeloned back to the right rear of Wauchope's 1st Brigade came Maxwell's with, to his right rear, Lewis's. Kitchener had moved the latter up in order to have MacDonald's more reliable Sudanese on the open flank of the echelon formation. Collinson was detailed to escort the transport along the river bank. MacDonald had been strengthened by the attachment of three batteries and eight Maxims but, in order to make way for Lewis to get into position, had first marched out westwards prior to wheeling into his place in the echelon of brigades. Consequently a gap developed between him and the other formations.

As the British crested the ridge and Maxwell's men began the climb up to Jebel Surgham itself, they came under fire from the summit. At the same time the noise of gunfire and musketry broke out far to the right rear. In the distance MacDonald's batteries could be seen in action and his battalions halted and deployed. Bearing down at great speed from the south-west came what had hitherto remained concealed and what the Lancers had failed to discover – the great horde of the Khalifa's reserve under his own black flag, Yakub's 17,000 warriors stretching from the western slopes of Surgham far out into the desert. Ahead of them stood only MacDonald's four battalions, with no troops nearer than Lewis's uncertain Egyptians half a

The charge of the 21st Lancers into the ambush laid by Osman
Digna. Colonel Martin, without a drawn sword or revolver, can
be seen at right, pointing. The officer on the grey, centre, may
represent Captain Kenna, who was awarded the Victoria Cross
for saving Lieutenant de Montmorency, assisted by Corporal
Swarbrick who gained the Distinguished Conduct Medal.
Painting by R. Caton Woodville.

Private James Byrne, 21st Lancers, who won the Victoria Cross for riding back into the mêlée, though twice wounded himself, to rescue the dismounted, disarmed and wounded Lieutenant Molyneux from imminent death.

mile away to his left and facing the wrong way, and the other all-Egyptian brigade down near the river a mile away.

Kitchener from Surgham at once perceived the danger into which the advance had placed MacDonald and accordingly sent out orders to change the front of his army from south to west. Maxwell was to wheel right and take up position across the summit of Surgham; Lyttleton was to form on Maxwell's left, Lewis on his right, while Wauchope was to double back and fill the gap between Lewis and MacDonald; Collinson and the Camel Corps were to move into position on MacDonald's right rear, facing north-west.

MacDonald, always calm in a crisis, opened fire at 1200 yards but his Sudanese, though unperturbed by the masses sweeping down upon them, were excitable and erratic in their aiming. Only by ordering them to cease fire and haranguing them for two minutes – though the Dervishes drew nearer with every second – could MacDonald achieve the disciplined musketry which he knew could alone save them. Many of the enemy fell but still they came forward. Then Kitchener's redeployment took effect and the brigades of Lyttleton, Maxwell and Lewis came over Surgham and into action, pouring their volleys into the Dervish right, forcing Yakub to detach men to confront this new threat. Now the tide began to turn, as the lethal power of modern weapons took its toll on the heroic massed charges of the enemy from the flank and in front. With the brigades from Surgham advancing firing, Yakub's right started to falter and break away into the desert behind.

To many of the Anglo-Egyptian infantry, viewing the heaps of enemy dead, it must have seemed that the Khalifa's army had spent itself and all that remained was the pursuit of a beaten foe. Some of the Dervishes still showed fight in front of MacDonald and his redoubtable men, who more than most were deserving of a respite. But at the very moment he was holding off Yakub's last assaults, he was again in deadly peril. Flooding down upon his rear from the Kerreri Hills came the hitherto uncommitted 5000 of Abd Allah Abu Siwar, supported in

Wauchope's British brigade advancing to support MacDonald's hard-pressed Sudanese in the final phase of the battle. This drawing, by Corporal Farquharson of 1st Seaforth, shows the left half of the brigade, Royal Warwicks and Camerons.

stages by Osman Sheikh-ed-Din's exhausted Mulazamin, returning from their fruitless pursuit of Broadwood. They were coming about half an hour too late for the Khalifa but they were coming nevertheless, 20,000 of them thirsting for revenge. Once more it was only MacDonald's 3000 who stood in the enemy path but again he was equal to the occasion. As the pressure from the south-west decreased, he shortened his line by degrees to form a new front facing north-west.

His right flank battalion, 9th Sudanese in column of companies facing south-west, wheeled to form line of companies facing the new threat, while his left flank, the 11th Sudanese in line, hastened across to form on the 9th's right, followed shortly afterwards by the 10th Sudanese, until only the 2nd Egyptians continued to face south-west. This manoeuvre was carried out under threat of attack from both directions and a heavy enemy fire, which caused 120 casualties in the twenty minutes it took to complete. However the brigade did not falter and each battalion opened fire on the approaching green flags as it came into line. But the brigade had been constantly engaged

for over half an hour, the excitement was again affecting the fire discipline and ammunition was running low. The batteries and Maxims ploughed furrows through the Dervish ranks but for all who fell, there were more behind, eager to win their entry into Paradise. Nearer and nearer they rushed until it looked as though it would come to hand-to-hand fighting. Reduced to about three rounds per man, the dauntless Sudanese infantry braced themselves with bayonets levelled. Suddenly help arrived on the right of the brigade.

Wauchope's brigade had been hurrying across the plain to fill the original gap on MacDonald's left, but it had over a mile to cover in intense heat, and by the time the panting men of the Lincolns in the lead reached their appointed position, Yakub's attack was broken. There could be no pause for rest as the Lincolns were at once ordered on another 700 yards at the double to assist MacDonald. The green flags

Dervish prisoners after the battle. The escorts are Northumberland Fusiliers.

were within a hundred yards of the 10th Sudanese when the leading company of the Lincolns, the old 10th Foot, formed line on their right, immediately opening a rapid independent fire across the front of the Sudanese. As the Lincolns' line was extended by their other companies, the firing changed to controlled volleys under which, at such close range, the last despairing onslaught of Mahdism checked, faltered and finally perished. A body of Baggara horse made one last wild charge, each rider seeking the death which most surely awaited him, and it was all over.

It was now 11.30 and, as the shattered remains of the Khalifa's mighty Ansar fled away across the desert to the west, Kitchener ordered the resumption of his interrupted advance on Omdurman. In the space of nearly five hours the Dervishes had launched four great mass attacks, each made with tremendous courage and the unflinching devotion inspired by religious fervour, but each had foundered under the destructive power of the bullet and the shell. The slaughter had indeed been horrific, nearly 10,000 Dervishes having been killed and countless thousands wounded. There were many in Kitchener's army whose respect for their enemy left them appalled by the dreadful heaps of dead and dying, and utterly thankful when the firing could cease.

Yet Kitchener had experienced some anxious moments. Had the Dervishes been able to co-ordinate their attacks better, particularly in the last hour and a half, and had Hector MacDonald not held firm, matters might have gone very ill, certainly for the Egyptian element of the army. Kitchener had much to be grateful for to the stalwart and phlegmatic ex-ranker, who only five years later was tragically to take his own life,[19] and to Broadwood, whose skilful action had resulted in the Dervish left wing joining the last attack too late. For many who had taken part, the victory was far less glorious than it was later made out to be by the British Press and public, while others, among them Captain Douglas Haig, felt that Kitchener's triumph owed more to luck than tactical ability. On the other hand, it had been gained at surprisingly little cost: only forty-eight had been killed — of which three officers and twenty-five soldiers were British — and 434 wounded. Of the regiments, by far the worst sufferers had been the 21st Lancers with seventy-one casualties, followed by the 9th Sudanese with forty. However, although the Battle of Omdurman had been won, the Khalifa had earlier fled the stricken field and no-one yet knew what might await them in his sprawling capital.

Left: The end of Mahdism. Dervish dead around the Khalifa's black standard. Drawn by H.C. Seppings-Wright.

[19] On account of an alleged homosexual offence committed when, as Major-General Sir Hector MacDonald, he was commanding in Ceylon.

15

Gordon Avenged

Later that afternoon Kitchener and his army entered Omdurman. Some slight resistance was encountered, but as soon as the population realised they were not to share the fate of many of the Dervish wounded out on the plain, who had been summarily despatched by some of the advancing army,[20] they thronged into the filthy streets to swarm excitedly round their conquerors, while a deputation formally surrendered the city to Kitchener. Any illusions of a triumphant progress through a fabled and mysterious Eastern city, that some of the British soldiers entertained, were quickly dispelled by the scenes of degradation, destruction and squalor, not to mention the stench, which greeted their entry. It seemed a poor reward for their labours and, after an exhausting day, most faced an unpleasant night, like Corporal Emery of the Rifle Brigade, who found himself bivouacking in a graveyard, full of 'dead donkeys, camels, horses and a good many other things'.

After returning from the battlefield, the Khalifa had taken refuge for a while in his palace but, warned of the approaching troops, made his getaway through a rear door, while the 13th Sudanese were battering down the main gate. Attached to Kitchener's Intelligence Department was Slatin Pasha, who had joined the expedition to identify and seize the man whose prisoner he had been for ten years. When he could find no trace of the Khalifa, Broadwood and his tired cavalry were sent off in pursuit. By then the Khalifa had reached the desert, heading into Kordofan to join still-loyal followers, and after a fruitless and difficult search for nearly twenty hours on insufficient food and water, Broadwood gave up the hunt and returned to Omdurman.

The Khalifa was never betrayed, his emirs and remaining troops stood by him, and for fourteen months he remained at liberty in Kordofan, planning his return. Eventually, in November 1899, a force under Wingate tracked him down, and in the ensuing fight the Khalifa and all his chief lieutenants were killed. Only Osman Digna, as might be expected, managed to escape but he too was later captured. Curiously the place where the Khalifa met his end was not far from Abba Island, where seventeen years before the Egyptians had first tried to capture the Mahdi. Other isolated pockets of resistance were sought out and eliminated by small Egyptian Army expeditions, but to all intents and purposes Mahdism had been crushed on the field of Omdurman.

For many Englishmen, and not least Kitchener himself, an underlying motive of the great endeavour had been the avenging of Gordon. On Sunday, 4 September, the Sirdar, his senior officers and representative detachments of every regiment crossed over the White Nile to parade before Gordon's ruined palace in Khartoum. The British and Egyptian flags were raised upon the roof. The Grenadiers' drums and fifes played the National Anthem, the band of the 11th Sudanese the Khedivial hymn. A 21-gun salute was fired from the *Melik*. More solemn music followed, the Guards with the 'Dead March in Saul', the Sudanese with the march from 'Scipio', after which came the memorial service, conducted by four chaplains. The Highland pipers played a lament, and finally the Sudanese band broke into a poignant rendering of what was believed to be Gordon's favourite hymn, 'Abide with me'. The normally harsh and stern Sirdar was seen to have tears coursing down his cheeks. As the plaintive

---

[20] Chiefly by Sudanese paying off old scores but some British were also culpable. In fairness to the troops, there were instances of Dervishes who, though wounded, were still highly dangerous, and others whose wounds were beyond hope of recovery.

notes drew to a close, there can have been few in that haunted place who were not moved by thoughts of how it must have been in those last, far-off days for the brave and lonely man who had never faltered in his duty. When a description of the ceremony reached the Queen at Windsor, she too wept as she wrote in her diary: 'Surely, now he is avenged;' a sentiment shared by many of her subjects.

A major factor that had impelled the British Government to undertake the re-conquest of the Sudan had been France's designs in Equatorial Africa to gain a hold over the head-waters of the Nile on which Egypt depended. Three days after the memorial service, news reached Kitchener that a European force had occupied Fashoda, four hundred miles south of Khartoum, in what theoretically was Egyptian territory. On the next day Kitchener set off up-

Kitchener's staff moving off towards Omdurman after the battle. The headquarters flag is carried by the man on the camel, while the Egyptian trooper on the grey holds up the Khalifa's black standard. Kitchener himself is at extreme left, riding out of the picture.

river with two companies of Cameron High-landers, the 11th and 13th Sudanese and five steamers. Ten days later he approached Fashoda to find the French tricolour flying and a Major Marchand with a small force of Senegalese sol-diers in possession. Marchand had arrived there in July after an epic march across 3000 miles of tropical forest and swamp which had begun two years before on the Atlantic coast. His mis-sion had been to take control formally of the country round the headwaters of the Nile which had been abandoned by Egypt (and con-sequently Britain) after 1885.

Grenadier Guards and Cameron Highlanders cheering the reading-out of the Queen's congratulatory telegram.

This confrontation between the armed representatives of two great European and Colonial powers deep in the middle of Africa was fraught with dangerous possibilities, particularly as Kitchener had the stronger force and was not usually noted for his tact. Fortunately both men liked and respected each other from the start, and Kitchener diplomatically wore the uniform of an Egyptian, not a British, general and flew the Egyptian flag from his steamers. He told Marchand that the French presence was a violation of Egyptian and British rights, and he protested at the French flag being hoisted in the Khedive's territory. Marchand replied that he was only obeying his Government's orders, that he could not withdraw without instructions from Paris and that, if Kitchener used force, he would be bound to resist and die at his post if necessary. Kitchener said he would hate to use force but he intended to occupy the whole Sudan; he then asked if Marchand had

authority to resist the raising of the Egyptian flag in re-assertion of the Khedivial sovereignty. Marchand admitted he was in no condition to do so. Kitchener thereupon had the Egyptian colours ceremonially hoisted, offered Marchand the use of his communications, and agreed to leave the tricolour flying until the dispute could be resolved by the interested Governments.

However in London and Paris no such harmony prevailed, and the bitter hostility between both countries over 'the Fashoda incident' and Egypt generally, grew to such intensity that war seemed a possibility. But after a while France — concerned about future German intentions and thus the need to acquire better relations with Britain, and also torn apart internally by the Dreyfus spy case — backed down and agreed, in March 1899, to a dividing line being drawn between British and French spheres of influence in Central Africa. This agreement marked the beginning of the end of France's long opposition to Britain's position on the Nile, which culminated in the Anglo-

French Agreement of 1904, under which France recognised Britain's status in Egypt in return for British recognition of France's in Morocco. This agreement, better known as the 'Entente Cordiale', was to alter dramatically the balance of power in Europe, as would be seen in 1914, and owed much to Lord Cromer's patient negotiation and wisdom.

Kitchener reached England at the height of the Fashoda crisis to receive a hero's welcome from Royalty, the Government, the Army and the public. He was raised to the peerage as Lord Kitchener of Khartoum, was awarded a GCB, the thanks of Parliament, a grant of £30,000, a costly ceremonial sword, a State banquet, and academic honours. A few months later, however, much of the enthusiasm turned sour when the Press, whose correspondents he had treated with contempt in the Sudan, revealed that after Omdurman he had ordered the desecration of the Mahdi's tomb and had proposed sending the Mahdi's skull to the College of Surgeons in London; to this were added allegations of his brutality to the Dervish wounded and the but-chery of civilians in Omdurman. This caused him considerable distress, and in due course a White Paper was published to refute the allegations, but by then he had returned to the Sudan as both Sirdar and Governor-General.

Egyptian rule was never fully restored over the Sudan. The British Government could not contemplate the dangers of returning the stricken country to the type of maladministration which had been the cause of all the troubles of the last seventeen years. Nor would the future well-being of the Sudan be helped by being tied to Egypt whose affairs, though vastly improved under Cromer's guidance, were still under financial shackles, and which legally remained the vassal of the Turkish Sultan. Clearly the task of bringing order and justice to the sorely-tried Sudanese people would have to be primarily a British responsibility, but on the other hand

A trooper of the 21st Lancers and Private Barnfield, Queen's Company, Grenadier Guards, holding up the telescope with which Gordon used to watch for the Relief Expedition in 1885.

Britain had no right to annex the country. A solution was therefore devised by Cromer, and an agreement drawn up in January 1899, whereby sovereignty over the Sudan was to be shared between Britain and Egypt in token of which 'the British and Egyptian flags shall be used together' throughout the country. Unlike her nominally advisory role in Egypt, Britain thus assumed a definite ruling function in the Sudan. The supreme military and civil command was to be vested in a Governor-General appointed by Khedivial decree on the recommendation of the British Government. By this formula was acknowledged the Khedive's former authority over the country, as well as Britain's claim, 'by right of conquest', to share in the system of administration and legislation that would have to be contrived, making 'due allowance ... for the backward and unsettled condition' of the reconquered provinces. Kitchener's methods as Governor-General may have been, in Cromer's understated phrase, 'perhaps a little more peremptory than is usual in civil affairs', but the Sudan Civil Service, which he founded, came in time to enjoy a reputation comparable to its Indian counterpart

Dervish guns captured in Omdurman. At extreme left is a Gatling gun.

for justice, sound administration and devotion to the welfare of the people.

Although in theory Britain and Egypt were equal partners in the reconstruction of the country, in practice, as Lord Lloyd wrote, 'the Sudan ship of state was to be officered by British, even if the warrant officers were Egyptian'. Moreover, so difficult did it prove, particularly in the early years of the Condominium to find Egyptians able and willing enough to serve in the Sudan, even as 'warrant officers', that the country was administered much as if it were a British colony. In any case, it was unlikely that the Sudanese, mindful of what they had suffered in the past from Khedivial rule, would have settled under an administration in which Egyptians predominated. As things turned out, the war-torn Sudan prospered under this novel arrangement, although in Egypt itself relations with Britain began to deteriorate not long afterwards owing to an Anglophobe Khedive and growing Nationalist sentiments, for which the Condominium became one of many resentments against the British presence.[21]

To the British public, still basking in a glow of Imperial euphoria engendered by the Diamond Jubilee of 1897, the re-conquest of the Sudan was a most gratifying episode and, when added to Cromer's great achievement in transforming Egypt from chaos into order and prosperity, was taken as further proof of the Empire's civilizing mission. By restoring tranquillity and security to the lands of one great waterway, the Nile – not to mention the rebuff to the old enemy, France – so had the other great waterway of the region, the Canal, been made safe for the continuance of Britain's Imperial task and the trade which financed it.

The overthrow of 'Fuzzy-Wuzzy' by the British soldier gained the Army fresh laurels to

[21] In 1914 the Khedive Abbas Hilmi threw in his lot with Turkey, and Egypt was declared a British Protectorate until 1922, when it became an independent sovereign state, subject to certain strategic requirements reserved by Britain. In 1953 it became a republic, and the British garrison, then confined to the Canal Zone, was withdrawn in 1956, the same year that the Sudan achieved its independence.

Above left: Obverse of the Khedive's Egyptian Star, dated 1882.

Above centre: Reverse of the Queen's Sudan Medal, 1896–98. To Private M. Hayden, Royal Irish Fusiliers.

Above right: Obverse of the Khedive's Sudan Medal 1896–1908, with bars 'The Atbara' and 'Khartoum'. To Private D. Smith, Royal Warwickshire Regiment.

add to those acquired not long before against Zulus and Afghans, enhancing its reputation and popularity in the eyes of a grateful public. The charge of the 21st Lancers at Omdurman, considered by George Steevens to be 'a gross blunder', was hailed as a great feat of arms, comparable with the Light Brigade at Balaclava, and immortalised on many a canvas. In recognition of its bloodstained two minutes of glory, the Regiment was designated 'Empress of India's' by Queen Victoria. According to *The Navy and Army Illustrated*, the return of the Grenadier Guards was 'the signal for an outburst of enthusiasm such as has not been witnessed in London for a great many years'.

Thousands lined the streets as the 'bronzed and weather-worn' troops marched from Waterloo Station to Wellington Barracks, where they were welcomed by the Duke of Cambridge. At Woolwich the 37th Field Battery was 'met with a reception, if anything, more hearty than that which greeted the Guards'. With men like these the safety of Nation and Empire seemed assured.

Yet what the Nation forgot, or did not care to recognise, was that the battle honours of ATBARA and KHARTOUM, soon to be emblazoned on regimental Colours, had been won by close-order formations using the Lee-Metford rifle, the Maxim gun and the Lyddite shell against primitive warriors armed largely with primitive weapons and employing primitive tactics. Within fifteen months of Omdurman, as well-aimed musketry from concealed and mobile marksmen crackled across the South African veldt, the Nation, its Empire and its Army were about to receive a very nasty shock indeed.

The British landing at Fashoda, 19 September 1898. Major Lord Edward Cecil, Kitchener's senior ADC, introducing Captain Keppel RN, commanding the gunboat flotilla, to Major Marchand before the Sirdar disembarked. Drawing by W.B. Wollen.

Appendix: Battle Honours and Medals

BATTLE HONOURS AND MEDALS

The following Battle Honours were awarded for the campaigns of 1882, 1884–85, and 1896–98: 1) EGYPT 1882. 2) TEL-EL-KEBIR. 3) EGYPT 1884 (First Suakin expedition). 4) NILE 1884–85 (Gordon Relief expedition). 5) ABU KLEA. 6) KIRBEKAN. 7) SUAKIN 1885 (Second Suakin expedition). 8) TOFREK. 9) HAFIR (Dongola expedition). 10) ATBARA. 11) KHARTOUM (Omdurman campaign).

These were awarded to the following regiments, present titles in *italics*:

1st Life Guards (1,2) * † *The Life Guards*
2nd Life Guards (1, 2) * † *The Life Guards*
Royal Horse Guards (1, 2) * † *The Blues and Royals*

4th Dragoon Guards (1, 2) * † *4th/7th Royal Dragoon Guards*
7th Dragoon Guards (1, 2) *4th/7th Royal Dragoon Guards*
5th Lancers (7) * † *16th/5th Queen's Royal Lancers*
10th Hussars (3) * *Royal Hussars*
19th Hussars (2, 3, 4, 5) *15th/19th King's Royal Hussars*
20th Hussars (7) * *14th/20th King's Hussars*
21st Lancers (11) * (as Hussars) *17th/21st Lancers*

Grenadier Guards (1, 2, 7, 11) * † *Grenadier Guards*
Coldstream Guards (1, 2, 7) * † *Coldstream Guards*
Scots Guards (1, 2, 7) * † *Scots Guards*

Northumberland Fusiliers (11) *Royal Regiment of Fusiliers*
Royal Warwickshire Regiment (10, 11) *Royal Regiment of Fusiliers*
Lincolnshire Regiment (10, 11) *Royal Anglian Regiment*

Royal Irish Regiment (1, 2, 4) *disbanded 1922*
Lancashire Fusiliers (11) *Royal Regiment of Fusiliers*
East Surrey Regiment (7) *Queen's Regiment*
Duke of Cornwall's Light Infantry (1, 2, 4) * † *Light Infantry*
Royal Sussex Regiment (1, 4, 5) *Queen's Regiment*
South Staffordshire Regiment (1, 4, 6) * † *Staffordshire Regiment*
Black Watch (1, 2, 3, 4, 6) * † *Black Watch*
Essex Regiment (4) * † *Royal Anglian Regiment*
Sherwood Foresters (Derbyshire) (1) *Worcestershire & Sherwood Foresters Regiment*
Royal Berkshire Regiment (1, 7, 8) *Duke of Edinburgh's Royal Regiment*
Royal West Kent Regiment (1, 4) * † *Queen's Regiment*
King's Shropshire Light Infantry (1, 7) *Light Infantry*
King's Royal Rifle Corps (1, 2, 3) * † *Royal Green Jackets*
Manchester Regiment (1) *King's Regiment*
North Staffordshire Regiment (9) *Staffordshire Regiment*
York and Lancaster Regiment (1, 2, 3) *disbanded 1968*
Highland Light Infantry (1, 2) *Royal Highland Fusiliers*
Seaforth Highlanders (1, 2, 10, 11) *Queen's Own Highlanders*
Gordon Highlanders (1, 2, 3, 4) * † *Gordon Highlanders*
Cameron Highlanders (1, 2, 4, 10, 11) *Queen's Own Highlanders*
Royal Irish Fusiliers (1, 2, 3) ** *Royal Irish Rangers*
Rifle Brigade (11) * † *Royal Green Jackets*

* Represented at 4), † represented at 5), and ** represented at 11) by a detachment only, hence ineligible for the honour.

The following regiments were represented at 4) and 5) by detachments only, hence ineligible for honours:

2nd Dragoon Guards * † *Queen's Dragoon Guards*

5th Dragoon Guards * † *5th Royal Inniskilling Dragoon Guards*

1st Royal Dragoons * † *The Blues and Royals*

2nd Dragoons (Scots Greys) * † *Royal Scots Dragoon Guards*

16th Lancers * † *16th/5th Queen's Royal Lancers*

3rd Hussars * *Queen's Own Hussars*

4th Hussars * *Queen's Royal Irish Hussars*

7th Hussars * *Queen's Own Hussars*

11th Hussars * *Royal Hussars*

15th Hussars * *15th/19th King's Royal Hussars*

18th Hussars * *13th/18th Royal Hussars*

Somerset Light Infantry * † *Light Infantry*

Royal Scots Fusiliers * † *Royal Highland Fusiliers*

Connaught Rangers * † *disbanded 1922*

Battle Honours were awarded to the following Indian regiments, 1922 titles in *italics*:

2nd Bengal Cavalry (1, 2) *2nd Royal Lancers, Gardner's Horse*

6th Bengal Cavalry (1, 2) *18th King Edward's Own Cavalry*

9th Bengal Cavalry (7) *Hodson's Horse, 4th Duke of Cambridge's Own Lancers*

13th Bengal Lancers (1, 2) *6th Duke of Connaught's Own Lancers, Watson's Horse*

Queen's Own Madras Sappers & Miners (1, 2, 7, 8) *Queen Victoria's Own Sappers & Miners*

7th Bengal Native Infantry (1, 2) *3rd/7th Rajput Regiment*

15th (Ludhiana) Bengal Native Infantry (7, 8) *2nd/11th Sikh Regiment*

17th (Loyal Purbeah) Bengal Native Infantry (7, 8) *disbanded 1922*

20th (Punjab) Bengal Native Infantry (1, 2) *2nd/14th Punjab Regiment*

28th Bombay Native Infantry (7, 8) *3rd Bombay Pioneers*

29th Bombay Native Infantry (2nd Baluch) (1, 2) *4th/10th Baluch Regiment*

MEDALS

THE VICTORIA CROSS

Gunner I. Harding, Royal Navy, HMS. *Alexandra*. At Alexandria, 11 July 1882.

Private F. Corbett, King's Royal Rifle Corps. At Kafr-ed-Dauar, 5 August 1882.

Lieutenant W.M.M. Edwards, Highland Light Infantry. At Tel-el-Kebir, 13 September 1882.

Captain A.K. Wilson, Royal Navy. At El Teb, 29 February 1884.

Quartermaster-Sergeant W.T. Marshall, 19th Hussars. At El Teb, 29 February 1884.

Lieutenant P.S. Marling, King's Royal Rifle Corps (Mounted Infantry). At Tamai, 13 March 1884.

Private T. Edwards, Black Watch. At Tamai, 13 March 1884.

Gunner A. Smith, Royal Artillery. At Abu Klea, 17 January 1885.

Captain N.M. Smyth, 2nd Dragoon Guards, attached Egyptian Army. At Omdurman, 2 September 1898.

Captain P.A. Kenna, 21st Lancers. At Omdurman, 2 September 1898.

Lieutenant Hon. R.H.L.J. de Montmorency, 21st Lancers. At Omdurman, 2 September 1898.

Private T. Byrne, 21st Lancers. At Omdurman, 2 September 1898.

Captain Hon. A.G.A. Hore-Ruthven, Highland Light Infantry, attached Egyptian Army. At Gedaref, 22 September 1898.

CAMPAIGN MEDALS

EGYPTIAN MEDAL, 1882–89

Obverse: Diademed head of Queen Victoria and legend 'Victoria Regina et Imperatrix'.

Reverse: The Sphinx with 'EGYPT' above, with date '1882' below; no date for later campaigns.

Size: 1.42 in. diameter.

Ribbon: $1\frac{1}{4}$ in. wide, three bright blue and two white stripes of equal width.

Bars: Alexandria, Tel-el-Kebir, El Teb, Tamai, El Teb-Tamai, Suakin 1884, Nile 1884–85, Abu Klea, Kirbekan, Suakin 1885, Tofrek, Gemaizah (1888), Toski (1889).

KHEDIVE'S EGYPTIAN STARS, 1882–91

Obverse: In the centre the Sphinx with three pyramids behind, all within a raised circle embossed 'EGYPT' followed by the applicable dates.

Reverse: The Khedive's monogram 'TM' within a raised circle.

Size: Bronze five-pointed star, maximum width 1.9 in.

Ribbon: $1\frac{1}{2}$ in. wide, plain dark blue.

Bar: Tokar (1891). Stars are dated 1882 (for 16 July – 14 September), 1884 (for 19 February – 26 March), 1884–86 (for 26 March 84–7 October 86). Undated stars for Suakin 1887 and on Nile in 1889.

QUEEN'S SUDAN MEDAL, 1896–98

Obverse: Crowned half-length figure of Queen Victoria and legend 'Victoria Regina et Imperatrix'.

Reverse: Winged figure of Victory, seated with palm and laurel branches in right and left hands respectively. At her feet 'SUDAN' on a plaque supported by three lilies. Behind her and on either side, the British and Egyptian flags.

Size: 1.42 in. diameter.

Ribbon: $1\frac{1}{4}$ in. wide, left half yellow, right half black, divided by $\frac{1}{16}$ in. red stripe.

Bars: Nil. (Medal awarded to those present at Firket, Hafir, Abu Hamed, Sudan 1897, Atbara, Omdurman).

KHEDIVE'S SUDAN MEDAL, 1896–1908

Obverse: In Arabic 'Abbas Hilmi The Second' and the Mahommedan year '1314' (1897).

Reverse: Oval shield bearing three stars and crescents in centre and surrounded by lances and flags. The whole superimposed on two crossed rifles and a cannon with a pyramid of six cannon balls. Beneath the whole, in Arabic, 'The Reconquest of the Sudan 1314'.

Size: 1.54 in. diameter.

Ribbon: $1\frac{1}{2}$ in. wide, broad blue stripe down centre, yellow on either side.

Bars: Firket, Hafir, Abu Hamed, Sudan (1897), The Atbara, Khartoum, Gedaref (1898), Gedid (1899), and six for subsequent small risings between 1900–1908.

Select Bibliography

Alexander, Michael, *The True Blue: the Life and Adventures of Colonel Fred Burnaby*, Hart-Davis, London, 1957.

Anglesey, Marquess of, *A History of the British Cavalry, 1816–1919, Vol III, 1872–1898*, Secker & Warburg, London, 1982.

Blunt, Wilfrid Scawen, *Secret History of the English Occupation of Egypt*, T. Fisher Unwin, London, 1907.

Bond, Brian (*ed*), *Victorian Military Campaigns*, Hutchinson, London, 1967.

Butler, Colonel Sir W.F., *The Campaign of the Cataracts*, Sampson Low, London, 1887.

Chevenix Trench, Charles, *Charley Gordon*, Allen Lane, London, 1978.

Childers, Lieutenant-Colonel Spencer, *The Life and Correspondence of the Right Honourable Hugh C.E. Childers, 1827–1896*, Two Vols, John Murray, London, 1901.

Churchill, Winston S., *The River War*, Eyre and Spottiswoode, London, 1899.

Churchill, Winston S., *My Early Life 1874–1908*, (1930), Fontana, London, 1959.

Cole, Major D.H., *Imperial Military Geography*, Sifton Praed, London, 1933.

Colvile, Colonel H.E., *History of the Sudan Campaign*, Her Majesty's Stationery Office, London, 1889.

Duncan, Lieutenant-Colonel B.A.C. 'Karari: The Battle of Omdurman', *British Army Review*, No. 74, London, 1983.

Gleichen, Count, *With the Camel Corps up the Nile*, Chapman & Hall, London, 1889.

Hamilton, General Sir Ian, *Listening for the Drums*, Faber, London, 1944.

Herold, J. Christopher, *Bonaparte in Egypt*, Hamish Hamilton, London, 1963.

Lehmann, John, *All Sir Garnet*, Jonathan Cape, London, 1964.

Lloyd, Lord, *Egypt Since Cromer*, Macmillan, London, 1933.

Magnus, Philip, *Kitchener: Portrait of an Imperialist*, John Murray, London, 1958.

Malet, Sir Edward, *Egypt 1879–1883*, John Murray, London, 1909.

Martin, Ernest J.(*ed*), 'Lincolnshires at Omdurman: Diary of Lieutenant H. Hodgson', *Journal of the Society for Army Historical Research*, Vol XXI, London, 1942.

Maurice, Colonel J.F., *Military History of the Campaign in Egypt 1882*, Her Majesty's Stationery Office, London, 1887.

Padfield, Peter, *Rule Britannia: the Victorian and Edwardian Navy*, Routledge & Kegan Paul, London, 1981.

Preston, Adrian (*ed*), *In Relief of Gordon: Lord Wolseley's Campaign Journal of the Khartoum Relief Expedition, 1884–1885*, Hutchinson, London, 1967.

St Aubyn, Giles, *The Royal George: The Life of HRH Prince George, Duke of Cambridge*, Constable, London, 1963.

Seaman, L.C.B., *From Vienna to Versailles*, Methuen, London, 1955.

Small, E. Milton (*ed*), *Told From the Ranks: Recollections of Service During the Queen's Reign by Privates and N.C.Os of the British Army*, Andrew Melrose, London, 1898.

Steevens, G.W., *With Kitchener to Khartoum*, Blackwood, Edinburgh, 1898.

Symons, Julian, *England's Pride: the Story of the Gordon Relief Expedition*, Hamish Hamilton, London, 1965.

Terraine, John, *Douglas Haig: the Educated Soldier*, Hutchinson, London, 1963.

Tylden, Major G., 'Tel-El-Kebir', *Journal of the Society for Army Historical Research*, Vol XXXI, London, 1953.

Tylden, Major G., 'The Camel Corps and the Nile Campaign of 1884–1885', *Journal of the Society for Army Historical Research*, Vol XXXVII, London, 1959.

Ward, S.G.P. (*ed*), 'Scots Guards in Egypt 1882: Letters of Lieutenant C.B. Balfour', *Journal of the Society for Army Historical Research*, Vol LI, London, 1973.

Weigall, Arthur E.P. Brome, *A History of Events in Egypt from 1798 to 1914*, Blackwood, Edinburgh, 1915.

Williams, Jeff, 'The Sudan 1885', *Sabretache – Journal of the Military Historical Society of Australia*, Vol XXIII, Canberra, 1982.

Williamson, J.A., *A Short History of British Expansion*, Macmillan, London, 1931.

Wingate, Major F.R., *Mahdism and the Egyptian Sudan*, Macmillan, London, 1891.

Wood, Field-Marshal Sir Evelyn, *From Midshipman to Field-Marshal*, Vol II, Methuen, London, 1906.

Wood, Field-Marshal Sir Evelyn, *British Battles on Land and Sea*, Two Vols, Cassell, London, 1915.

Woods, Frederick (*ed*), *Young Winston's Wars: Original Despatches of Winston S. Churchill, War Correspondent, 1897–1900*, Leo Cooper, London, 1972.

Ziegler, Philip, *Omdurman*, Collins, London, 1973.

Various Regimental Histories

PERIODICALS

The British Empire (1972)

The Graphic (1884–85)

The Illustrated London News (1882, 1884, 1885, 1898)

The Illustrated Naval and Military Magazine (1884–85)

The Navy and Army Illustrated (1898)

Soldiers of the Queen – Journal of the Victorian Military Society (1982)

Picture Credits

Index